HIDDEN QUEST

KNOWING GOD THROUGH CREATION

Hide and Seek Ministries

Hidden Treasure Quest: Knowing God Through Creation
ISBN 13: 978-0-9994901-0-5 (paperback); 978-0-9994901-1-2 (ebook)

Copyright © 2017 by Hide and Seek Ministries

Published by Hide and Seek Ministries
Republic, MO 65738
www.hideandseekministries.com

Library of Congress Control Number: 2017956948

Printed in the United States of America

HIDDEN TREASURE QUEST

Proverbs 2:1-11

My son, accept my words.
Store up my commands inside you.
Let your ears listen to wisdom.
Apply your heart to understanding.
Call out for the ability to be wise.
Cry out for understanding.
Look for it as you would look for silver.
**Search for it as you would search
for hidden treasure.**
Then you will understand how to have
respect for the LORD.
You will find out how to know God.
The LORD gives wisdom.
Knowledge and understanding come from his mouth.
He stores up success for honest people.
He is like a shield to those who live without blame.
He guards the path of those who are honest.
He watches over the way of his faithful ones.
You will understand what is right and honest and fair.
You will understand the right way to live.
Your heart will become wise.
Your mind will delight in knowledge.
Good sense will keep you safe.
Understanding will guard you.

(NIrV, emphasis added)

CONTENTS

PARENTS, CAREGIVERS, AND LEADERS

Who is Hidden Treasure Quest for?

Hidden Treasure Quest is a Christian discipleship series written for ages nine to fourteen. These flexible books can be read independently, as a family, during homeschool, or in a small-group study with multiple ages.

Why Hidden Treasure Quest?

Due to cultural influences and a lack of discipleship, a countless number of youth and young adults are abandoning their faith. *Hidden Treasure Quest* guides young readers to develop their **own** relationship with the Lord. God's plan for all people is much more than saying a prayer to get to heaven. Every follower of Christ is called to be a disciple and to make disciples. The *Hidden Treasure Quest* series helps readers learn how to apply God's Word to their lives and learn how to follow and live for Jesus.

How should Hidden Treasure Quest be read?

The series of books are best read in order. With the suggested bible reading plan, memory verses, and scripture references, it is encouraged that the reader have access to a Bible in a version that the reader can understand. A master list of memory verses and the bible reading plan for each chapter can be found near the back of this book. The master lists also contain *additional* bible verses for those who are interested in further bible study. A printable version of these lists is available at www. hideandseekministries.com. Although not required, the *Hidden*

Treasure Quest Study Guide can also be utilized to facilitate an even deeper understanding and help readers learn how to study the Word of God more efficiently and effectively.

A Note About the Science Chapters

The science chapters found near the end of the book (chapters 15-17) are a great way to help readers understand the similarities and differences when comparing textbook science and the Bible. The chapters will also help students discover biblical answers to questions that result from a science-related class that teaches about evolution and/or the big bang theory.

The information provided has intentionally been presented in an easy-to-understand way. However, if the reader is too young to understand the concepts found in the first two science chapters, *Hidden Treasure Quest* can easily be read and understood by skipping chapters 15 and 16. You will find this book to still be very beneficial if the reader needs to save those two chapters for when they are ready for them.

The Hide and Seek Ministries' (HSM) Website

The HSM website provides additional resources for Christian discipleship including fun facts, bible quizzes, answers to bible questions, and free printable worksheets. To find out more, visit www.hideandseekministries.com.

TIPS FOR THE READER

Bible Reading Plan and Memory Verses

At the beginning of every chapter in this book, you will find bible verses to memorize and other verses to read in your Bible. These reading and memory verses are encouraged but not required to understand each chapter. There are two lists near the back of this book (pages 119-128) that have all the bible verses for every chapter. These lists also have *additional* bible verses for those who are interested in further bible study.

Bible References

The information in this book comes from the Bible. You will often see a bible book name, chapter, and verse(s) number in parenthesis at the end of a sentence. This shows where you can find the information in your own Bible. The book name will be abbreviated. Here is an example:

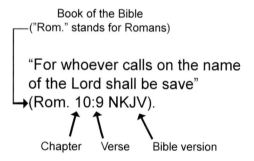

You will only see the Bible version (like NKJV or NIrV) when the sentence is exactly how it appears in the Bible (meaning this book is quoting the Bible word-for-word). If you don't see the version, then the sentence has summarized what the bible verse says. You may find a list of abbreviations for the books at the beginning of most Bibles.

Daily Reading

For many reasons, we should fill our heart with God's Word. Each of us should spend time reading the Bible every day. If you struggle doing this, there are many great bible reading plans available to help you stay on track. Reading plans give you a list of verses you should read each day. Some help you read the Bible in one year or less. Others will take you through part of the Bible in a year. Pick one that works for you and stick with it. You should continue to follow a plan even after you have finished *Hidden Treasure Quest*. Most bibles have a reading plan included in them. You can also find free plans on the internet (with the assistance of your parents). See Appendix A for more tips to understand the Bible.

Make a Journal

As you read the Bible each day, try making a journal. Copy down a bible verse in your notebook that stands out to you. Then write notes about that verse such as what the verse means, and how you can do what it says. Copying verses from the Bible on another piece of paper is always a great idea. It will cause you to read the verse more slowly and think about what it says. In addition to taking notes, you can also make a list of verses that you want to memorize. You can record a list in your journal to practice every day. The memory verses in this book are a great starting point.

INTRODUCTION: A NOTE FROM BEN

My name is Benjamin, but everyone calls me Ben. On the outside, I may appear to be an average thirteen-year-old boy who loves swimming, reading, and exploring with my dog. But on the inside, I'm not average at all. In fact, I'm much different than most people in the world. Before I tell you more about me, I want to tell you about my friend named Nate.

Nate's favorite thing to do as a kid was to go sailing with his grandfather. Every Saturday morning, Nate loved the smell of salt water and feeling the wind on his face as they sailed for hours on a warm summer day. In Nate's eyes, nothing was better than gliding on a massive white boat and learning from the world's best sailor. He enjoyed it so much that Nate decided he wanted to have a sailboat of his own. At an early age, Nate began to save every penny he could. By the time he was an adult, he had finally saved enough money to buy his very own boat.

Nate was so excited the day he brought it home. It was white with dark blue stripes on the side that seemed to sparkle in the sun. It was the most beautiful sailboat he had ever seen. The following Saturday, Nate prepared for his first sailing adventure by himself. With his grandfather in mind, he worked all morning inspecting above and below deck to ensure his boat was ready for the ocean water. With everything in place, he finally began to untie the rope to set sail. Suddenly, Nate realized something that made him panic. He did not know how to sail his boat by himself. He had always enjoyed sailing but had never taken the time to learn more than just the basics of how to sail. Nate had relied on his grandfather to do most of the work.

Like Nate, some of us have not taken the time (or maybe have not had the chance) to learn more than just the basics of believing in God. Nate had been around sailing all his life. He had learned several things about it from watching his grandfather. However, when he grew older and didn't have his grandfather helping him, he wasn't prepared to do it by himself.

Maybe you have learned a few things about God or even several things. Maybe you have learned many bible stories about Adam and Eve, Noah's ark, David and Goliath, or Samson. But do you really know God in a way that you are prepared to live your whole life following Jesus? We don't want to make the same mistake Nate did and be unprepared.

I believe that God is real, the Bible is true, and Jesus died to save my life from sin. This is what makes me so different than many other people in the world. I have been made a child of God, but I have found that many people do not believe the same way. Some people have made fun of me for believing in God. Others have tried to tell me that God is not real. Some think there is a God but say He is different than what the Bible describes. Many people even think we came from apes and the earth was made from a big explosion!

Some of my friends ask me questions about my faith in God, and I don't always have the answer. I don't like it when I don't know what to tell them. This is why I am here today. I want to introduce you to *Hidden Treasure Quest*. *Hidden Treasure Quest* was designed to help young people learn about God with their heart, not just their mind.

In the Bible, Proverbs 2 talks about searching for wisdom, knowledge and understanding like we would a hidden treasure. These things can only come from God. Wisdom, knowledge, and understanding can help us make the right choices and know God in a close, personal way. As you start searching for the things of God like you would a hidden treasure, you will see that God is actually easy to find. He is waiting for you to look for Him, and He's even excited about it! The *Hidden Treasure Quest* series is designed to help you become prepared to live your life following Jesus.

There will never be a time when we know everything there is to know about God. However, there are so many things we can know right now. In this first book, we will be learning the ways of God by looking at what He has created and learning how and why He created it. I will be making comments along the way to help you understand some things. You will know it's me when you see my picture:

You will see my comment below my picture like this.

Oh, I almost forgot. This is my dog, Checkers. You will see him from time to time. He follows me everywhere I go.

READ:
Genesis 1
Genesis 2

WHY DID GOD CREATE PEOPLE?

Memory Verse:
So God created man in His own image.
Genesis 1:27 (NKJV)

I'm going to ask you to think about two different people.

Person number one: Think of a person you know a lot about. Maybe it's your mom, dad, brother, sister, or someone else who lives with you. Imagine that person in your mind. What is something this person enjoys doing? What is their favorite food or favorite color? Do you know how they act when they are happy? Do you know something that makes them excited or mad? Do you know if they like animals, like the outdoors, or like any sports?

Person number two: Now think about a person that doesn't live with you. You know their name, but you don't spend much time with them. Maybe it's a neighbor, a person at church, or school. Imagine that person in your mind. Try to answer the same questions for this person.

🧍

Why is it easier to answer questions for the person you live with and see every day? It is easier because you have a *relationship* with that person. Having a relationship with someone means you know a lot about them. You know that person in a close, personal way. It's more than just knowing their name and a few facts about them. A relationship connects you with another person. You have a lot better relationship with your parents (or the people you live with) than a neighbor that lives down the road. The more time you spend with someone, the better relationship you will have with them. Your relationship is so strong with your parents (or other relatives) that you not only know a lot about them, but you love them.

Did you know we can have a relationship with God? God is the Creator of the universe and all living things. God's most special creation of all is people. Out of all the great wonders in the world, people are His greatest treasure! Having a relationship with God is the reason He made us. He did not make us because He was lonely or needed people to help Him. He made us out of love and wants to have a relationship with each one of us.

As God was preparing to make Adam, the first man, He said, "Let us make mankind in our image, in our likeness..."

2

(Gen. 1:26 NIV). Creating us in His *image* means God made us to be like Him. This does not mean that He was making another god, and it doesn't mean that we look exactly like Him. But on the outside, in many ways, we look like God. We don't look like sharks or rhinos or spiders. Although God is a spirit and does not have lungs to breathe, He created us to look like Him.

We are also made in His *likeness*. This means we have certain qualities and abilities that other creation does not have. Have you ever seen a dog eat something? Maybe you have accidently dropped a piece of food on the floor and your dog snatched it and ate it. Dogs don't take time to enjoy their food. They usually swallow the whole thing in one gulp. Can you imagine if we all ate and drank like dogs? Picture your whole family sitting at the dinner table with their face in a bowl of food gulping it down. Then, when you were thirsty, you started lapping up water with your tongue.

People are God's only created beings who were made in His likeness and image. God made us *unique,* and He did it for a reason. God made us to be like Him so we have the ability to have a relationship with Him. Unlike animals, people can talk, think, reason, and make choices. God wants us to choose to spend time with Him and get to know who He is. He loves us and wants us to love Him. He wants us to be able to enjoy knowing Him, and He wants to spend eternity (forever) with us in heaven.

Your relationship with God is the most important relationship you will ever have. The first step to having a relationship with God is believing in His Son, Jesus Christ. Jesus said, "I am the way and the truth and the life. No one comes to the Father except through me" (John 14:6 NIV). Only those who choose to believe in Jesus can have a relationship with God.

In order to know God, you also must spend time with Him. Like any relationship, the more time you spend with Him the better you will know Him. Even though we can't see Him with our eyes, God is always with us. We can spend time with Him by talking to Him (praying) and reading His Word (the Bible).

Let's say you were in the same room all day with your best friend. You sat right next to him all day, but you never said a word to each other. You didn't even look at each other. That is what we are doing to God if we don't speak to Him all day. God is always with us and waiting to hear from us. He wants to talk with you because He loves you.

It's important that we don't just know facts about God, but we know Him in a close, personal way. But is this even possible? Can we learn about someone we can't see with our eyes? The Bible says, *Yes! Hidden Treasure Quest* is a series of discipleship books to help you know God through creation, Jesus, and the Holy Spirit.

What is *discipleship*? A disciple of Christ is not just referring to the twelve people that followed Jesus while He was on earth. *You* can also be a disciple. In fact, some of Jesus' last words before He went to heaven told each person to go into all the world and make disciples (Matt. 28:19). Jesus tells us to *be*

4

a disciple and to *make* disciples.

Believing in Jesus does not automatically make you a disciple. Being a disciple of Christ means God is most important in your life. You have a desire to seek and follow Jesus with all your heart, even if it means you are different than most other people in the world. As a disciple, you make a choice to live *for* Jesus. You also desire to find and follow *His* plan for your life. *Hidden Treasure Quest* is designed to help you become a disciple of Jesus Christ. Discipleship is an exciting and rewarding journey!

✝

MORE THAN A BODY

Memory Verse:
For we live by faith, not by sight.
2 Corinthians 5:7 (NIV)

When I was nine years old, I decided to accept Jesus as my Savior. I was so excited to start a new life and begin a relationship with God. A few days later, Checkers was watching me play soccer in my backyard. We were having fun until my sister came outside. She quickly told me I wasn't kicking the ball correctly. I could feel the anger growing inside me. Without much thought, I shoved her in the middle of the back. She fell forward and started crying. Instantly, I felt bad. And I was also confused. I was told that when I believed in Jesus I was made into a new person and my sins were washed away. So why was I still sinning if I was made new?

Body, Spirit, and Soul

God created every person to have three parts. We are made of a body, a spirit, and a soul (1 Thes. 5:23). The Bible can be hard to understand if we do not know who we are. Let's look at some of the differences between our three parts.

1. Your Body

It is easy to see that every person has a body. It is what you see when you look in a mirror. Your body is much like a house for your spirit and soul. When a person chooses to believe in Jesus, their body does not change. If they were a boy before they first believed in Jesus, they will still be a boy afterward.

Your body will not live forever like your spirit and soul. We can see that our bodies are not perfect right now. However, for all who go to heaven, Jesus will one day transform our bodies to be perfect like His (Phil. 3:21).

2. Your Spirit

We are created in God's image (Gen. 1:26). God is a spirit (John 4:24), and each person He created is also a spirit. We are a spirit with a body and a soul.

7

Your spirit can either be dead or alive. Sin makes your spirit dead (Eph. 2:1,5; Col. 2:13). Every person is born with sin (Ps. 51:5), and sin separates you from God. If your body dies while your spirit is dead in sin, you will go to hell (Rom. 8:9).

However, Jesus makes your spirit alive. When you believe in Jesus, *you become a new person in your spirit* (2 Cor. 5:17). Your spirit is made new and alive (Eph. 2:1). It is called being "born again" (John 3:1-21). You are not born again as a baby, but you are born of God and become a child of God (John 1:12). Being born again means your spirit no longer has sin. Your new spirit is righteous, holy, and perfect just like Jesus (Eph. 4:24; 1 John 4:17).

A born-again spirit is so perfect that it will *not* need to be changed when you go to heaven. The spirit you have after believing in Jesus is the same spirit you will have in heaven. The real you is your spirit and soul. Your current body is temporary and will pass away. But your spirit and soul will live forever.

Remember, having a perfect spirit does not mean that your body is perfect. It does not mean you will never sin again. Sins are things we do that God says is wrong. Lying, stealing, cheating, and not honoring your parents are examples of sin. The Bible says that all people have sinned (Rom. 3:23). Jesus was the only perfect person to live on earth. However, when you sin, your spirit is still perfect. *Sin cannot change your spirit.*

This does not mean that we can do what we want and not care if we sin. When we truly believe in Jesus and love Him, we will *want* to listen to Him (1 John 2:3-6). We should not keep sinning on purpose (Heb. 10:26). The Bible says, "We can be sure that we know God if we obey his commands" (1 John 2:3 NCV). Doing what God's Word says is *proof* that we are saved and believe in Jesus, but it is not *how* we are saved. We are saved only by believing in Jesus. It is a free gift from God and is not based on what we do (Eph. 2:8).

3. Your Soul

The third part of you is your soul. Your soul includes your mind, emotions, will, and conscience. Your soul is where you learn, make choices, have feelings, and have thoughts. Your soul lives forever just like your spirit. But it is *not* immediately changed when you believe in Jesus. However, it can and should be changed.

If you spend time studying the Bible, the way you think can be changed to match the Word of God (Rom. 12:2). The Bible can change your soul (your thoughts, emotions, feelings, and desires) to be more like Jesus. But this change will not happen instantly like the change with your spirit. It takes time, and you must *choose* to change your soul through God's Word.

You May Not Feel Different

Everyone can look in a mirror and see that they have a body. If someone taps you on the shoulder, you can feel it. You know that to step on something sharp feels bad. And you know that a soft, fuzzy blanket feels good when it's cold. You can feel things that happen to your body very easily.

You can also feel things in your soul. You know when you are happy, sad, angry, afraid, or excited. Your soul can even be hurt if someone says unkind words to you. However, you

9

cannot feel things in your spirit. The Bible says you are a new creation when you trust in Jesus (2 Cor. 5:17). But what if you don't "feel" new? What if you feel the same as you felt before you believed? This can be confusing if you don't understand that you cannot feel your spirit.

For example, the Bible says when you believe in Jesus you have the same power inside you that raised Jesus from the dead (Rom. 8:11). If you don't understand that you can't feel your spirit, you may wonder where this power is. The power is still available to you even though you can't feel it in your spirit.

When you understand your body, spirit, and soul, you can begin to understand who you are as a believer in Jesus. You can't just rely on what you feel. God's Word is the only way to find out what your spirit is like. When you look in the Bible, it is like you are looking into a mirror for your spirit.

The Spiritual World

In the book of 2 Kings, it tells about a man named Elisha. He was a prophet of God. A prophet is a person who gives people messages from God. The king of Syria was trying to start a war with Israel (God's people). Every time the king would make plans to attack, Elisha would warn Israel to stay away. Elisha was ruining the plans of the king. Finally, the king found out what Elisha was doing, and he sent a large army to find Elisha.

One morning, Elisha's servant got up early and saw a huge army with horses and chariots surrounding them. The servant was frightened and asked Elisha what they should do. Elisha told him, "Don't be afraid...Those who are with us are more than those who are with them" (2 Kings 6:16 NIV). But the servant looked around and saw only two of them, and he saw thousands of soldiers ready to attack them. He likely thought, *how could there be more of us when I count only two?*

Then Elisha prayed and said, "Open his eyes, Lord, so that he may see." The Bible says, "Then the Lord opened the servant's eyes, and he looked and saw the hills full of horses and chariots of fire all around Elisha" (2 Kings 6:17 NIV). The servant's eyes had not been closed. He was looking around with his eyes the whole time. God allowed the servant to see what was happening in the *spiritual* world. There were only two of them in the *physical* world (or the world they could see with their eyes). But there were thousands of angels in the spiritual world that they could not see with their physical eyes.

The spiritual world is very real. God, angels, Satan, and demons are in the spiritual world (see also Col. 1:16, Eph. 6:12). We cannot see this world by looking with our physical eyes unless God allows us to. While you are reading this sentence, you may have at least one angel sitting next to you. This is a great thing!

The Bible says that God has assigned angels to help and serve those who believe in Jesus (Heb. 1:14). If Elisha and his servant didn't realize this, they could have seen the huge army surrounding them and tried to escape in fear. Instead, they had confidence in God's army of angels and were victorious over their enemies. In every situation we face, we must remember that there is more happening than what we can see, hear, or feel. Just as it was for Elisha and his servant, what happens in the spiritual world is more important than what we see in the physical world.

The Real You

Remember, we are made of a body, spirit, and soul. When you believe in Jesus, your spirit is the only part that is made perfect. And your spirit is the only part that you *cannot* feel. So, you must look in the Bible to see what your spirit is really like.

God looks at you and sees your perfect spirit. When you believe in Jesus, you are made a child of God (Gal. 3:26). God loves you just as He loves His Son, Jesus. Don't be afraid that God will stop loving you every time you sin. "If we confess our sins, he will forgive our sins" (1 John 1:9 NIrV).

When you put your faith in Jesus, don't think of yourself as a sinner anymore. Don't call yourself a sinner. Look at yourself the way God looks at you. You are the righteousness of God (2 Cor. 5:21), and God loves you no matter what happens!

✝

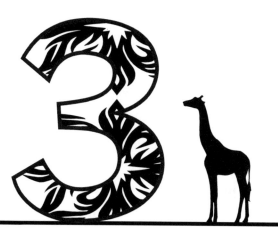

READ:
Psalm 145
Psalm 146
Psalm 147

OUR PERFECT CREATOR

Memory Verse:
In the beginning was the Word, and the Word was with God and the Word was God. John 1:1 (NKJV)

The word creation means all the things that God has made. When we say God created the earth, it means He made the earth. We have already read about why God created people. In the next several chapters, we are going to start learning about God by looking at how and what He has created.

God is Eternal

The book of Genesis is the first book in the Bible. It tells us about the perfect world that God made. Even though the Bible starts out by saying, "In the beginning", this was not the beginning for God. God does not have a beginning or an end. He was there before He created the universe and before the Bible was written (Ps. 90:2). God is what the Bible calls *eternal* (Deut. 33:27, Rom. 16:26). God was never born. He has always been alive and always will be alive. This can be hard to imagine, but it's true!

God is Perfect and So Was His Creation

Can you imagine if we lived in a perfect world? There would be no sickness, pain, or sadness. No one would be poor or be treated badly. There would be no fear, worry or making mistakes. Even though it may be hard to imagine, there was a time when everything was perfect. In the beginning, God created everything to be perfect just as He is perfect (Matt. 5:48). After the six days of creation, "God saw everything that He had made, and indeed it was very good" (Gen. 1:31 NKJV). For a time, Adam and Eve enjoyed the perfect world that God created.

God Never Changes

God never changes. God is exactly the same as He was when He created the universe. He hasn't grown any older and hasn't become any smarter. It is impossible for Him to change. He has always been perfect and cannot be any more perfect. He also cannot be any less perfect. He will never be stronger or weaker. He will never have more knowledge or more wisdom. He has all there is to have. The Bible says He "is the same yesterday and today and forever" (Heb. 13:8 NIrV). Psalm 102 (verses 25-27 NCV) says:

14

In the beginning you made the earth, and your hands made the skies. They will be destroyed, but you will remain. They will all wear out like clothes. And, like clothes, you will change them and throw them away. But you never change, and your life will never end.

God's Understanding Does Not End

One day as I was playing with Checkers, I started thinking about all the animals in the world. Did you know that even the smartest people on earth have no idea how many different species of animals there are? They have been trying to figure out the number for many years but cannot do it. Scientists guess there are millions, but no one knows for sure. Well, except for God. He knows everything.

Did you know that God cannot learn? He already knows all there is to know. God knows the answer to any question you can possibly think of. He knows everything that has happened in the past and what will happen in the future. He knows every thought you have and every word you say. He even knows how many hairs are on your head (Luke 12:7). He knows how many stars are in the sky and the names of each one (Psalm 147:4). He knows all things because He is the One who made it all. The smartest person in the world does not come close to knowing what God knows (1 Cor. 1:25). The Bible says God's "understanding is infinite" (Ps. 147:5). In other words, God's knowledge goes on forever; it never ends! The Bible says in Isaiah 40:25-26 (NCV):

> God, the Holy One says, "Can you compare me to anyone? Is anyone equal to me?" Look up at the skies. Who created all these stars? He leads out the army of heaven one by one and calls all the stars by name. Because he is strong and powerful, not one of them is missing.

God is Three Persons in One

God was not alone, in a sense, when He was creating everything. In Genesis, God said, "Let **Us** make man in **Our** image, according to **Our** likeness..." (Gen. 1:26 NKJV emphasis added). If God was alone during creation, then why did He use the words *Us* and *Our* instead of *Me* and *My*? The book of John helps us find part of the answer. It says, "In the beginning was the Word, and the Word was with God, and the Word was God" (John 1:1 NKJV). The "Word" John is talking about is Jesus. If we read the same verse again, and replace "the Word" with "Jesus", it would say this: In the beginning was *Jesus*, and *Jesus* was with God, and *Jesus* was God.

The next two verses go on to say, "He was in the beginning with God. All things were made through Him..." (John 1:2-3 NKJV). Jesus was with God in the beginning when God created all things. Not only was Jesus there, but the world was made *through* Him. The Holy Spirit was also with God during creation. The Bible says before God created light, "the Spirit of God was hovering over the face of the waters" (Genesis 1:2 NKJV).

If we look at John 1:1 again, it also says that Jesus *is* God. These verses help show us that God is three persons in one. God is:

1. God, the Father
2. God, the Son (Jesus)
3. God, the Holy Spirit

God as three persons is often called the *Trinity* or the *Godhead*. Jesus is the Son of God, and He is also God. The Holy Spirit is the Spirit of God, and He is also God. Just as God has always been alive, so has Jesus and the Holy Spirit. However, there is still only *one* God; one God as three persons.

✝

READ:
Daniel 1
Daniel 2:1-23

THE POWER OF GOD'S WISDOM

Memory Verse:
The Lord made the earth by his power. He used his wisdom to build the world and his understanding to stretch out the skies. Jeremiah 51:15 (NCV)

When I look up at the stars at night, I wonder how long it would take to travel to one of them. Last summer, we traveled to my uncle's house that was 600 miles away. It took us ten hours to get there. It seemed like it took forever. Traveling to a star is more than I can imagine. It's hard to think about how big our universe is. In fact, scientists don't even know how big it really is. They can only guess at its size. But there is One who does know...and it's not Checkers!

God's Power and Wisdom

God has all power. There is nothing that is more powerful than God. When we look at what God has created we can see how powerful He is. The Bible says, "The Lord made the earth by his power. He used his wisdom to build the world and his understanding to stretch out the skies" (Jer. 51:15 NCV). God created everything with His power, wisdom and understanding.

The *universe* is everything that God created under heaven. This includes the earth, stars, other planets, moons, and everything in between. A *galaxy* is a huge group of stars, dust, and gas. There are billions of galaxies in the universe.[1] The *Milky Way* is the name of the galaxy that Earth is in. There are hundreds of billions of stars in our Milky Way galaxy alone. But when we look up at the sky at night, we can only see a few thousand of those stars.

Let's estimate that there are 200 billion stars in the Milky Way.[2] That is so many stars that if you counted each star, one second at a time, it would take you about 3,171 years to count them all! That is just the stars in *one* galaxy. There are billions more galaxies in the universe.

The size of the Milky Way galaxy is enormous. It is about 590 trillion (590,000,000,000,000) miles across.[3] Remember, that is just one galaxy out of billions more. It is so big that it takes about eight minutes for the light of the sun to reach earth. Earth is like a little tiny speck in the vastness of space.

What about all the stars in *all* the galaxies? Let's say some scientists are correct and there are about 100 billion galaxies with each having about 100 billion stars. It would take you over 317 trillion (317,000,000,000,000) years to count all the stars in the universe. There are 12 zeros in that number! That's not the number of stars, that's *years* to count them!

Maybe you think that 317 trillion years would take too long. So, let's ask seven billion people to help us count. With each person counting their part of stars, it would still take one person about 45,300 years to count their portion! Only God knows the exact number of stars and has a name for each one.

How big do you think the universe must be to hold billions and billions of stars? The closest star to earth (besides the sun) is about 25 trillion (25,000,000,000,000) miles away.[4] If we could drive (in a pretend flying outer space car) going an average speed (about 60 miles per hour), it would take us over 47 million years to get there without stopping. And that is traveling to the closest one. That's a long time without a bathroom break!

God is in All Places at Once

One night, I was in a play at church. At the same time, my cousin was playing in his first baseball game. My grandmother wanted to watch us both, but she could not be in two places at once. God, however, can be in more than one place at a time. In fact, He is everywhere all at the same time.

Wherever you are God is there. Even in our huge universe, there is no place where God cannot see or hear you. And when He is with you, He is also with everyone else in the world at the same time. You can never escape His presence. If you were to swim to the bottom of the ocean, God would still be there. If you could travel to a star, God would be there too. And if you were on a star, you would not be any closer to God than if you were on Earth. You cannot travel anywhere to get closer to God or farther away. He is closer to you than your own thoughts. "Nothing in all creation is hidden from God's sight" (Heb. 4:13 NIV).

There is not a time when God will say: *Sorry, I am too busy to help you right now.* Or, *You are too far away from Me to help you.* God doesn't sleep (Ps. 121:4). He is always there (day or night) ready to speak to you, bless you, protect you, guide you, and provide you with everything you need. Let's read Psalm 139 (vs. 1-10,15-18 NIrV):

Lord, you have seen what is in my heart.
You know all about me.
You know when I sit down and when I get up.
You know what I'm thinking
even though you are far away.
You know when I go out to work
and when I come back home.
You know exactly how I live.
Lord, even before I speak a word,
you know all about it.
You are all around me, behind me and in front of me.
You hold me safe in your hand.
I'm amazed at how well you know me.
It's more than I can understand.
How can I get away from your Spirit?
Where can I go to escape from you?
If I go up to the heavens, you are there.
If I lie down in the deepest parts of the earth,
you are also there.
Suppose I were to rise with the sun in the east.
Suppose I travel to the west
where it sinks into the ocean.
Your hand would always be there to guide me.
Your right hand would still be holding me close...
None of my bones was hidden from you
when you made me inside my mother's body.
That place was as dark
as the deepest parts of the earth.
When you were putting me together there,
your eyes saw my body even before it was formed.
You planned how many days I would live.

You wrote down the number of them in your book
before I had lived through even one of them.
God, your thoughts about me are priceless.
No one can possibly add them all up.
If I could count them,
they would be more than the grains of sand.
If I were to fall asleep counting and then wake up,
You would still be there with me.

✝

READ:
Exodus 19
Psalm 19

THE POWER OF GOD'S GLORY

Memory Verse:

The heavens tell about the glory of God. The skies show that his hands created them. Psalm 19:1 (NIrV)

If someone had never seen a basketball before, you could describe it to them. You could tell them it is a hard ball filled with air and made of leather or rubber that is usually red-like in color with black stripes. You can describe how you bounce it on the ground or throw it to another person. You could even use your hands to show its size.

However, using words to tell about God can be much harder. God is more than what our words can describe. The Bible says the sky tells about God's glory (Ps. 19:1). God's glory can be hard to describe in words. But the Bible does give us many examples to help us understand.

What is God's Glory?

God's glory is God's way of showing people who He is. God is a spirit and does not have a body like we do. But when God reveals His glory, we can "see" Him and learn about Him. God's glory includes His beauty, power, goodness, and truth. The definition of glory in the Bible also refers to abundance (or a very large amount that is more than enough). God has so much glory that we will never see all there is. Believers will spend eternity learning new things about God. However, there are many things we can know about God right now. And God revealing His glory to us is one way we can learn and believe.

God Reveals His Glory Through Creation

From the beginning of the world, God has revealed His glory through creation. The Bible says, "The heavens tell about the glory of God. The skies show that his hands created them" (Ps. 19:1 NIrV). We can look at the sky and see God's glory: His beauty, power, goodness, and truth. The sky shows God's glory throughout the entire earth (Is. 40:21, Ps. 19:1-4).

God's glory "speaks" to us without words (Ps. 19:3). In the book of Acts, it says:

> Turn to the living God. He is the one who made the heavens and the earth and the sea. He made everything in them...he has given proof of what he is like. He has shown kindness by giving you rain from heaven. He gives you crops in their seasons. He provides you with plenty of food. He fills your hearts with joy (Acts 14:15,17 NIrV).

25

By looking at what God has made, we can see God's kindness and His desire to make us happy and give us what we need. We can learn about God by recognizing His glory.

God Reveals His Glory Through Signs

There are other ways that God reveals His glory. Many times, God revealed His glory to the Israelites. The Israelites were God's special group of people. He rescued them from being slaves in Egypt and promised to take them to a special land. As God rescued them and led them through the wilderness, He did many amazing things. The Bible says God rescued them with "tests, signs, miracles, war, and great sights, by his great power and strength" (Deut. 4:34 NCV). God brought plagues on the Egyptians, parted the Red Sea, appeared in clouds and fire, provided food from heaven and water from a rock, drove away enemies, and did many other amazing wonders.

When God gave the Israelites the ten commandments, His glory appeared on a mountain as fire (Ex. 19:18). His glory brought fire, smoke, a thick cloud, and thick darkness (Deut. 5:22). It shook the mountain and there was a loud trumpet sound with thunder and lightning (Ex. 19:16). His presence was so powerful that the Israelites could not touch the mountain or they would die (Ex. 19:12). God used signs like these to show the Israelites His glory (Num. 14:22).

God Shows His Glory Through Light

God's glory is not only found in fire and clouds. Another way God reveals His glory is through light. For instance, there is no sun in heaven because God's glory provides all the light that is needed (Rev. 21:23).

A second example is found through Moses. After Moses talked to God, God's glory made Moses' face glow (Ex. 34:29-35; 2 Cor. 3:13). The glow was so powerful that the Israelites were afraid to come near him. Moses had to cover his face with a veil as He spoke to them.

Ezekiel's vision is another example of God showing His glory through light. Ezekiel was a priest and a prophet. God showed Ezekiel visions of heaven, and he saw the throne of God. Ezekiel said God's glory looked like a bright light and a glow that seemed like a "rainbow in the clouds on a rainy day" (Ez. 1:28 NIrV).

God Only Reveals a Part of His Glory

God shows His glory in many different ways. But when we see His glory, we are only seeing a small part of who God is. Moses said to God, "Please, show me Your glory" (Ex. 33:18 NKJV). God agreed to have His glory pass by Moses, but God allowed Moses to only see His back and not His face. God's glory is so powerful that God said to Moses: "You cannot see My face; for no man shall see Me, and live" (Ex. 33:20 NKJV). God showed Moses *part* of His glory.

Right now, we only see a reflection (or likeness) of God's glory. The Bible says it is like we are looking in a dim (or unclear) mirror (1 Cor. 13:12). But someday we will clearly see God's glory in heaven and see Jesus face to face.

God's Glory Shows that He is God

Only God can be compared to the likeness of fire, lightning, clouds, thunder, a rainbow, and light. God's glory is powerful and amazing! God's glory reveals that He is the one true God. There is only one God, and no one else is like Him. He is the Creator of all things. He is above all, knows all, has all power, and is in all places at once. "His name alone is honored. His glory is higher than the earth and the heavens" (Ps. 148:13 NIrV).

In the Bible, we read that God spoke to Job out of a storm. God's words remind us of His glory, and that He alone is God. God said:

> Where were you when I laid the earth's foundation?
> Tell me, if you know.
> Who created the ocean?
> Who caused it to be born?
> Job, have you ever commanded the morning to come?
> Have you ever shown the sun where to rise?
> Have you traveled to the springs at the bottom of the ocean?
> Have you walked in its deepest parts?
> Do you understand how big the earth is?
> Tell me, if you know all these things.
> Where does light come from?
> And where does darkness live?
> Have you entered the places where the snow is kept?
> Have you seen the storerooms for the hail?
> Where does lightning come from?
> Where do the east winds live that blow across the earth?
> Who tells the rain where it should fall?

Who makes paths for the thunderstorms?
Can you bring out all the stars in their seasons?
Can you lead out the Big Dipper and the Little Dipper?
Do you know the laws that govern the heavens?
Can you rule over the earth the way I do?
Can you give orders to the clouds?
Can you make them pour rain down on you?
Do you hunt for food for mother lions?
Do you satisfy the hunger of their cubs?[1]

God Gave His Glory to Jesus

God's glory is not just found in fire, clouds, and light. God's glory is also in His Son, Jesus Christ. God gave His glory to Jesus (Is 42:5-8). Jesus came to earth as a human (and as God) to save us from our sin. The Bible says when people saw Jesus, they saw God's glory (John 1:14).

Jesus revealed God's glory through healing and miracles. Jesus did miracles that people by themselves could not do. These miracles revealed that Jesus was sent by God, is the Son of God, and the Savior of the world. Jesus made the blind see, the deaf hear, and the lame walk. He fed thousands of people with little food and commanded storms to stop. He walked on water and cast out evil spirits. When Jesus performed miracles, He revealed God's glory (John 2:11, 17:4).

However, Jesus shows us only a glimpse of God's glory. In the book of John, it says, "There are many other things Jesus did. If every one of them were written down, I suppose the whole world would not be big enough for all the books that would be written" (John 21:25 NCV).

29

God shows us His glory though creation, through His signs and wonders, and through Jesus. He does this so we might know more about Him, know that He is God, believe in His Son, and have eternal life. The Bible says, "But these are written so that you may believe that Jesus is the Christ, the Son of God. Then, by believing, you may have life through his name (John 20:31 NCV).

✝

READ:
Luke 1:1-25
Luke 1:57-66

THE POWER OF GOD'S WORDS

Memory Verse:
For the word of God is living and powerful, and sharper than any two-edged sword. Hebrews 4:12 (NKJV)

Think of what the world would be like if no one could speak. We would need a lot of paper to write down what we wanted to say. But what if there were no words at all? Imagine going to a football game or to school and no one said a word the entire time. Imagine going to a restaurant, but you couldn't speak to order food. How could someone buy a house, sell a car, or get a job without using words? There would be no books, computers, radio, television, or phones. There are a lot of things we cannot do without words. Words are very important, and they are also very powerful.

31

God's Words Created All Things

God created everything by speaking words (Heb. 11:3). God spoke to *nothing* and made *something* out of it. God spoke to darkness and said, "Let there be light" and light appeared (Gen. 1:3 NIrV). He didn't use His hands to shape the animals or trees. He didn't build the mountains with a hammer. He didn't get a pail of water to fill the oceans. God spoke it and it was done. Creation shows the power of God's words.

What is God's Word?

The Bible is God's words written down in a book. When talking about the Bible, some might say *God's words, God's Word, the Word of God,* or *Scripture.* It all means the Bible. Working through the Holy Spirit, God inspired over 40 different people what to write. Those writings ended up being 66 different books. Those books were put into *one* book called the *Bible.* The Bible is divided into two parts: the Old Testament and the New Testament. The Old Testament tells of the times before Jesus came to earth. The New Testament starts at the time of Jesus' birth and tells what happened afterward.

The first time the words in the Bible were recorded, they were written in the languages of Hebrew, Greek, and Aramaic. The Bible was later translated (or put into other languages) so other people could read it too. Today, the Bible is still not translated into all the languages of the world. Although it has been translated into thousands of languages, there are still millions of people who do not have the Bible translated into their own language.[1]

To better understand the Bible, it sometimes helps to study the meaning of the words in the original language. For example, in the Greek language, God's *Word* is described in two different ways.

1. **logos** [pronounced lō'-gōs] = the written Word of God
2. **rhema** [pronounced ray'-mah] = the spoken word

God's *written* word and the *spoken* word work together. The written word (the *logos* or the Bible) has God's power. But that power is not released until it is spoken (*rhema*). The words that are in the Bible first came from the mouth and heart of God (2 Tim. 3:16; Matt. 12:34). That is what makes the written Word so powerful. However, just because you carry your Bible with you does not mean that the pages and typed letters are going to bring power. The power comes when you believe in and *speak* what is written on those pages.

Think about walking into a room and turning on the light. You flip the switch and the light turns on. The reason the light turned on is because you flipped the switch. However, power for the light does not come directly from the switch. The power comes from a power plant that likely uses fossil fuels to make electricity. You can *use* the power by flipping the switch, but the power does not come from the switch alone.

Likewise, the power of God's words comes from the Bible (God's written Word). It's like the power plant. And we use that power when we *speak* His written Word (like flipping the switch for the lights).

Understanding how God's Word should work in our lives is very important. God wants us to read and understand His Word. He wants us to put His Word into our heart, protect it, believe it, and speak it so He can give us all the things we need. Because it is so important, we will talk more about God's Word in the next few chapters.

✝

READ:
Proverbs 1
Proverbs 2

HOW TO HEAR GOD'S WORDS

Memory Verse:
Faith comes by hearing, and hearing by the word of God.
Romans 10:17 (NKJV)

During lunch, my dad calls my mom every day. When my mom answers the phone, my dad does not have to say, "Hello. This is your husband, Philip." She knows it is him just by the sound of his voice. My mom and dad spend a lot of time together and know each other very well. They have a close relationship which makes it easy for them to recognize each other's voice.

If we want to hear God, we need to have a relationship with Him. We need to know more than just some facts about Him. We need to know Him in a close, personal way so we can recognize His voice.

God is Speaking to You Right Now

Every time you read the Bible God is speaking to *you*. The words were not just written for the people who lived thousands of years ago. God wrote the Bible knowing that you would one day read it. He put words in the Bible that He wanted you to read. Every word in the Bible is for *you*. The Bible was written many years ago, yet God had you in mind when He inspired the authors to write it. He knew each word you would need to read in order to help you throughout your life.

God Speaks Through the Bible and the Holy Spirit

God's Word can make good things happen in your life. The Bible helps us receive salvation. It can also help us make decisions, see our prayers answered, and make Satan leave us alone. His Word can bring healing to our whole body. His Word can also help us receive blessing and give us wisdom, encouragement, comfort, peace, and joy.

The Bible also helps us know God. As you continue to read the Bible, you will learn many exciting Bible stories (all of which are true). But you will also start learning things about God. As you keep reading, God will start showing you things about Himself. He wants to show you who He is. He wants you to know Him like you know your best friend or someone in your family (only much more than that).

As you develop a relationship with God, you will hear Him speak to you (even when you're not reading the Bible). When you believe in Jesus, God gives you His Spirit to live inside you, and He never leaves you. God speaks to you through the Holy Spirit. You may not hear a voice aloud, but you will be able to hear Him speaking to you on the inside. However, we must learn how to recognize His voice. If you don't take time to know God, you won't be able to hear Him speak.

Learn to Recognize God's Voice

Gods says you must seek Him with all your heart (Jer. 29:13). This means you must make Him most important in your life. Spend time reading His Word every day. The more you search His Word, the more you will understand and know Him. Take time every day to go to a quiet place to read the Bible, pray, and listen. As you read, you will learn about God and get to know Him in a close, personal way. It may not happen right away, but eventually the Holy Spirit will make God's Word come alive to you. You will recognize God's voice. You will understand His words and know what to do. You will know in your heart that the words on the page are for you. Don't give up after the first few tries. Building a relationship takes time.

Does this mean you can open the Bible and it will tell you whether you should play soccer or baseball this year? It may seem helpful if God would make bright yellow, flashing signs with arrows that said things like: *Go this way! Don't do that! Get this job! Go to this school! Stay away from this person!* However, if He did that it would almost be too easy.

God wants us to *want* to know Him. He gives us the *choice* to know Him. He doesn't force us to do anything. He wants us to seek and find Him. We must make an effort. Once you do, you will see that He is not hard to find. But we do have to try.

There are too many things in this world that pull us away from God, and knowing Him will not happen automatically.

Although the Bible may not say something like, "I want you to play soccer this year", the Holy Spirit will guide you in making those kinds of decisions. But you must be listening and be able to recognize His voice. If you take the time to know God, it is not hard to do. He wants you to learn about Him, and He wants you to hear His voice. Keep reading, praying, and seeking Him. Don't give up. God is waiting for you to find Him. In fact, He is really excited about it!

Here are some examples that will help us understand.

1. Zack was scheduled to fly on a plane in the afternoon. But he kept getting a horrible feeling about flying. He prayed about the feeling, and it would not go away. It was not fear, but something was just not right. He finally decided to cancel his flight. Later that night, Zack found out the plane had crashed. That feeling Zack had was the Holy Spirit speaking to him, and he was so thankful he had listened. If Zack did not know God well enough to recognize His voice, he may have gotten on the plane. The feelings we have are not always from God. Especially feelings like fear and worry. Fear and worry do not come from God. Zack,

however, had taken the time to know God and was able to recognize His voice.

2. Jill had several friends at school and she enjoyed spending time with them. However, her friends sometimes did things that Jill knew was wrong. Jill didn't want to lose her friends, so she did what they did. One day, Jill was reading her Bible and she read the words, "Don't live the way this world lives" (Rom. 12:2 NIrV). When she read these words, she felt something on the inside of her. It was like she knew God was speaking these words to her. And she knew that He was talking about the things she did with her friends. Jill knew she had to start acting differently and maybe even find new friends. It wasn't something she was excited about. But after she listened to God, she was so thankful that she did. Jill didn't realize her old friendships were keeping her from knowing God more and being blessed by Him. Jill took the time to listen and was able to recognize the Holy Spirit speaking to her.

3. Every morning James got up early to pray. Sometimes while he was praying, James would see something with his eyes closed. It was like he was having a short dream while he was awake. What James saw were visions from God. The Bible says that God will give people dreams and visions to tell them things (Joel 2:28). This doesn't mean all dreams are from God. Probably most of the dreams you have are not. James had a relationship with God and could recognize when God was speaking to him through a vision or dream.

God's Words Give Wisdom and Understanding

The Bible is filled with God's wisdom, knowledge, and understanding. God's Word is like a light that helps us see. We don't have to stumble through life as if we are walking in the dark. God's Word helps us make the right decisions, and it helps us develop a relationship with God. God is the only One that knows the past, present and future. He knows everything about you. He knows exactly what will make you happy and exactly what you need and want. God *wants* to help you with the power of His Word.

God has plans for your life (Eph. 2:10, Jer. 29:11). Those plans are much better than any plan you could make on your own. But there is no way to know those plans unless you spend time reading and listening to His Word. It doesn't matter how big or how small the decision is. He *will* help you. We should search in His Word like we would search for a hidden treasure. In Proverbs, it says (2:1-12 NIrV):

> My son, accept my words.
> Store up my commands inside you.
> Let your ears listen to wisdom.
> Apply your heart to understanding.
> Call out for the ability to be wise.
> Cry out for understanding.
> Look for it as you would look for silver.
> Search for it as you would search for hidden treasure.
> Then you will understand how to
> have respect for the Lord.
> You will find out how to know God.
> The Lord gives wisdom.

Knowledge and understanding come from his mouth.
He stores up success for honest people.
He is like a shield to those who live without blame.
He guards the path of those who are honest.
He watches over the way of his faithful ones.
You will understand what is
right and honest and fair.
You will understand the right way to live.
Your heart will become wise.
Your mind will delight in knowledge.
Good sense will keep you safe.
Understanding will guard you.
Wisdom will save you from the ways of evil men.
It will save you from men who twist their words.

✝

READ:
Psalm 1
Proverbs 3

USING GOD'S WORDS

Memory Verse:
If you declare with your mouth, "Jesus is Lord," and believe in your heart that God raised him from the dead, you will be saved. Romans 10:9 (NIV)

God's Word Gives Us Faith and Salvation

Let's say you have a best friend that you see every day. You talk, laugh, and do everything together. You take care of each other and are excited to be together. You always look forward to seeing your best friend. But one day something happens. A huge wall is built, and its length goes as far as you can see. You are on one side and your best friend is on the other. There is no way to climb it and no way to knock it down. It is so big that even if you yell at your friend, he still can't hear you. Now you're alone and must do everything on your own.

Although there isn't a real wall, it helps us understand what sin did. God made Adam and Eve, and He put them in the

42

perfect world that He created. However, Adam and Eve chose not to listen to God and sin entered the world. Everything was no longer perfect. Sin put a separation between people and God. With sin, we can't have a relationship with God and we can't be with Him in heaven.

Now, every person born is born with sin (Rom. 3:23). God says the punishment for sin is death. This means sin will cause a person to be separated from God in hell forever. God does not want this for anyone. So God sent His Son, Jesus Christ, to earth to take the punishment for us. Jesus was the only One that could take it away. Jesus died on the cross (instead of us), broke the "wall" of sin, and God raised Him from the dead.

When we put our faith and trust in Jesus, we are forgiven of our sin and we are no longer separated from God. But where do we get our faith? God's Word! God's Word gives us the faith we need to believe in Jesus and be saved from sin (called salvation) (Rom. 10:17). The Bible says, "If you declare with your mouth, "Jesus is Lord," and believe in your heart that God raised him from the dead, you will be saved" (Rom. 10:9 NIV). We use the power of God's Word to be saved from sin.

1. We hear God's Word.
2. We believe God's Word in our heart.
3. We speak God's Word with our mouth.

You hear, believe, and speak. After you hear and believe, you *say* what you believe. You may say something like this:

43

Jesus, I say today that You are my Lord and Savior. I believe in my heart that God raised You from the dead. I ask you to forgive me of my sins. By having faith in your Word, I receive salvation. Thank you for saving me.

Receiving salvation is like a story of a man who owed a king some money. The king decided to bring every person before him who owed him something. One man came before the king and owed him millions of dollars. It didn't matter how hard the man tried, it was too much money to pay back. The king told his guards to throw the man in jail for the rest of his life. But before the guards took the man away, another man walked into the room.

This man said, "I will give you a choice. You can choose to go to jail or you can receive a free gift. If you choose to take the gift, you won't owe the king any money and you are free to go. But that's not all. With the gift, if you choose to be different than the rest of the world, I will give you wonderful things throughout your life." The man continued, "If you need something, just ask me, and I will give it to you. I will do everything to take care of you. You can talk with me every day, and I will give you great joy. Someday, I will take you to a wonderful place that is perfect. It is free of sickness, fear, and worry. And you will get to stay there with me forever."

The guilty man said, "What must I do to receive this free gift? I am not a good person and do not deserve it."

The man responded, "This gift is available to anyone. It does not matter what kind of person you are or what you have done. The key to receiving the gift is in my words. Hear my words, believe my words, and then speak my words. Then the gift is yours. After you receive the gift, you will be made a new person on the inside."

Jesus is offering the free gift of salvation. He took away sin and saved us from the punishment of hell. His gift allows us to have a relationship with God. And we receive His gift by hearing, believing, and speaking **His words**. Jesus is the only way to God and to heaven. No one deserves His gift, but He still offers it to all people. By believing in Jesus, we become a new creation and receive God's spirit inside us. We are made children of God. God's Word is powerful! The second book in the *Hidden Treasure Quest* series explains much more about what Jesus did for us. We will continue to talk more about God's words in the next few chapters.

CHOOSING YOUR WORDS

Memory Verse:
Your tongue has the power of life and death.
Proverbs 18:21 (NIrV)

I really like listening to different bird calls. All bluebirds have their own bluebird sound. Cardinals make sounds that only cardinals make. However, a bird called a Superb Lyrebird is different. These birds learn and repeat sounds they hear from other birds and humans. They have even learned how to make the sound of a car alarm, a chainsaw, and a camera shutter.

The lyrebird is so good at copying the sounds they hear, they can fool the birds they are copying. If a lyrebird makes a sound like a Whipbird, a real Whipbird can be tricked into thinking he is hearing sounds from his own kind.

What's even more amazing is the lyrebird can teach its children the sounds it has learned. So, if a mother lyrebird knows how to sound like a chainsaw, she can teach her babies how to do the same.

God made people with the ability to speak. And, like a lyrebird, we sometimes tend to repeat what we hear. But we have a choice what we say and when we say it. And we have a choice what words we repeat. Many don't realize that the words we speak are very important. We should be very careful about what words we choose to use.

Our Words Are Important and Powerful

The Bible says every word we say comes from our heart (Matt. 12:34-35). If you find yourself saying things that you shouldn't, it's because there are things in your heart that shouldn't be there. Those things enter your heart through your eyes and ears. If you spend time listening to bad music, watching bad television, or spending time with people who speak bad words, those words will enter your heart and you will end up repeating them. The Bible says that one day, when Jesus returns to earth, we will all have to give a reason for every careless word we have said (Matt. 12:36). If we say something that we shouldn't have, we will one day have to give a reason why we said it.

Furthermore, our words have power. We were created in the image and likeness of God (Gen. 1:26). You are not God, but you are made similar to Him in many ways. Unlike animals, we have the ability to do things like God does. God speaks and things happen. We speak and things also happen. The Bible says that our mouth leads our whole body (James 3:2-5). In the Bible, James gives an example of a ship. He says a ship has a rudder. A rudder is a small piece of wood or metal and, when it is turned, it steers the whole ship. In the same way, our tongue is a small part of our body. Our whole body listens to what our mouth says. With our words, we direct the course of our lives.

If you keep saying, "I am really horrible at math", then you will likely struggle to do math. If you continue to say, "I love to eat", then you will find yourself eating more and more (which is not always a good thing). Proverbs 12:18 says "wise words bring healing" (NCV). If you continue to say, "I always get sick", what do you think will happen? We lead our life with our words, and you will end up doing what you say (Prov. 23:7).

Our emotions (or feelings) also come from our words (Prov. 15:23). If we are always complaining and talking negatively, we will find that our own feelings are unhappy. But if we are speaking positive words with thanksgiving and kindness, we will have feelings of happiness and peace.

We have a choice of what words we use and we should choose carefully. The Bible says, "The tongue has the power of life and death..." (Prov. 18:21 NIrV). We can choose to speak life (good), or we can choose to speak death (bad). To speak life as God speaks life, we need to fill our hearts with His Word. However, if we pay more attention to things in this world, we will find that our words are changed based on what we hear and see. The things we hear and see get into our hearts, and then we will speak them. We will start speaking things that have a negative impact on our lives. Be sure to speak words that match God's Word. Remember, the words you say can also enter other people's ears and affect *their life* as well.

Remember, we must hear, then believe and speak. Look at an example with me. Let's say my family needs a car.

*1. **Hear** – I hear from the Bible that God will provide for all my needs. In Philippians, it says, "My God will meet all your needs" (4:19 NIrV).*

*2. **Believe** – Then I believe in my heart that He will help us with our needs. I memorize the verse from Philippians to get it in my heart.*

*3. **Speak** – Then I pray (or speak) to God and say something like, "Lord, Your Word says that you will provide for all my needs. You know that we need a car and I ask you to help us get one. Thank you for helping us."*

Because I spoke God's Word in my prayer with faith, they are powerful. But the words I speak about the situation after I pray are also powerful.

*1. **To speak life** – As I talk to others, I might say, "I know God has answered my prayer." Or I might say, "When God helps us get a car, a lot of things will be much easier." Even though I may not have a car yet, I have faith that He has answered my prayer and I will get one. The words I speak come from the faith that is in my heart.*

49

*2. **To speak death** – As I talk to others, I might say, "Well, I prayed for a car. We will see if I get one." Or I might say, "It's been a while since I prayed. I don't know if God is going to answer my prayer after all." This is speaking death over the situation. My words are coming from what I see with my eyes and not faith that should be in my heart. These words and thoughts of unbelief may cause me not to get a car. It's not God's fault but my own for not having faith and speaking life.*

Faith in God's Words

In the book of John, it says, "If you remain in me and my **words** remain in you, ask whatever you want, and it **will be** done for you (15:7 NIrV emphasis added). If we follow Jesus (making Him most important), and we fill our heart with His Word, then we will ask for what *we want* and it will be done. It doesn't say *maybe* it will be done. It says it *will be* done. God wants to give us things that we want. We can receive His promises through His powerful words. In the book of Mark, it says:

> "Have faith in God," Jesus said. "What I'm about to tell you is true. Suppose someone says to this mountain, 'Go and throw yourself into the sea.' They must not doubt in their heart. They must **believe** that what they **say** will happen. Then it will be done for them. So I tell you, when you pray for something, **believe** that you have **already received** it. **Then** it will be yours (Mark 11:22-24 NIrV emphasis added).

50

The Bible says that God's Word is "settled in heaven" forever (Ps. 119:89 NKJV). This means God's Word is final in heaven. When God says something, He expects it to happen. He didn't say, "Let there be light" and then say, "Well, we will see if it happens." God said, "Let there be light" and there was light (Gen. 1:3). What God says in heaven is exactly what happens.

In order for God's words to happen on earth, we must first believe and speak His words. *Then* it will be done. This is called faith. Faith is not based on what we see with our eyes. We must believe God's Word more than the things we see. We must believe we have *already* received what we prayed for, even though we don't yet see our prayer answered with our eyes. We believe God heard our prayer, answered it, and we will see it with our eyes soon.

The words we speak after we pray show what is in our heart. Choose your words carefully. God expects His words to happen. We should also expect His words to happen in our own life when we use them with faith.

✝

PROTECTING GOD'S WORD

Memory Verse:
Above everything else, guard your heart. Everything you do comes from it. Proverbs 4:23 (NIrV)

Every spring I help my grandfather plant a garden in his backyard. We plant (or sow) things like carrots, cucumbers, and lettuce. Each plant starts as a seed, and it takes a lot of work to get the soil ready for the seeds. We must get rid of the weeds and rocks because they can keep the plants from getting the nutrients they need. After the soil is ready, we carefully place the seeds in the ground. We must make sure we water and take care of them, so they will grow and produce the food that I love to eat.

God says His words are like seeds. They can be planted in our heart, and we must take care of them so they will grow. If we do, they will produce fruit. This means God's promises, that are found in the Bible, will happen in our life and we will see our prayers answered.

When Jesus was on earth, He told stories called *parables* that had important messages and helped people learn about God. One parable Jesus told was about a sower (or a farmer). A sower is a person who scatters seeds on the ground so they will grow food. The parable teaches us how to receive and protect God's Word so it will grow and produce great things. You can read the parable in Matthew 13, Mark 4, and Luke 8.

In the parable, the sower puts seed on four different types of ground. But only one type of ground allows the seed to grow and produce fruit. The seeds are stolen from the other three types of ground. The sower put seeds on:

 1. **The wayside** (or a path). But the birds came immediately and ate all the seed. The seed didn't have a chance to be planted or grow.

 2. **Rocky ground**. There was not much soil in the rocky ground and the seeds could not grow strong roots. The seeds grew for a short time, but the sun caused the plants to die and no fruit was produced.

53

3. **Thorny ground**. Seeds were planted with thorns. They started to grow, but the thorns choked and crowded out the plants so they made no fruit.

4. **Good ground**. The seeds were planted, they sprang up, and they grew fruit. They produced "a crop 30, 60, or even 100 times more than the farmer planted" (Mark 4:8 NIrV). They grew more fruit than the number of seeds that were planted.

The Meaning of the Parable

The Seed is

God's Word

The Sower is

God
(or someone who speaks His Word)

The Ground is

a Person's Heart

The Wayside

The wayside is like a person who hears God's Word, but they don't pay attention to it. Satan comes *immediately* and takes the Word from their heart. His Word doesn't have a chance to do anything for the person. For Satan, this is most important to him. He doesn't want God's Word to grow and produce God's power in your life. Satan knows God's power is far greater than his own.

Rocky Ground

 The rocky ground is like a person who hears God's Word, and they gladly receive it in their heart. However, they only believe God's Word for a short time. Since God's Word is in their heart, hard times or problems come to try to take it away. Then when a problem happens, that person starts speaking words that are opposite of what God's Word says. The person may say something like, "Bad things always happens to me," or, "I just don't think this will ever get better." They might even say, "Maybe God is trying to teach me a lesson." A person who speaks something *different* than the Word of God allows Satan to steal God's Word from their heart. That person will not produce fruit in their life.

Instead, they should be speaking God's Word if a problem comes to keep Satan from stealing it. *God, I know you will help me. I know that God will provide everything that I need. I know that God's power inside me is far greater than Satan. Satan, I command you to leave me alone, in Jesus name.*

The Thorny Ground

 The ground with thorns is like a person who hears God's Word and it goes into their heart. However, other things also enter their heart and they crowd out God's Word. No fruit is produced. For example, being worried or scared crowds out God's Word. Also, if a person thinks about money in a wrong way, it also crowds out His Word. And if a person spends time

wanting things that are not good for them, those things enter in their heart and crowd out God's Word also.

Things that crowd out God's Word enter your heart through your eyes and ears. Therefore, we must be careful what we watch and hear so we protect our heart. When we allow these things to enter our heart, Satan is able to steal God's Word from us. If you find yourself worried or scared, remember it is not from God. It is Satan's way to try to steal God's Word from you. If this happens, you should speak God's Word and make Satan leave so he cannot steal from you. Satan has to listen to God's Word (James 4:7).

The Good Ground

 The good ground is like those who hear God's Word, accept it, and it grows and produces fruit. This is the kind of heart that God's wants everyone to have. But it's our choice. It does not happen on its own. God's Word will produce fruit in your life *if* you protect your heart from Satan. However, it takes time for seeds to grow. We sometimes must be patient. While we are waiting, we must continue to read the Bible and choose not to be like the rest of the world. God's Word can crowd out the things that are not supposed to be in our heart and keep Satan from stealing from us. Seeds will grow *if* you take care of them.

When God's Word grows and produces fruit, that's when God's power is released in your life. God's Word is always the same. It always has the same power. However, it doesn't work for everyone. Many people do not take the time to make good ground in their heart. This is why some people are not saved from sin. And this is why some people don't receive God's promises or answered prayers. They allow Satan to steal God's Word from them.

Jesus said we must understand the parable of the sower so we can understand all His other parables. This parable shows how the kingdom of God works. We need to learn how to make our hearts the good ground. If you are seeing fruit in your life (your prayers are being answered and God's promises are happening), then your heart is good ground.

But notice in the book of Mark it says there was "a crop 30, 60, or even 100 times more than the farmer planted" (Mark 4:8: NIrV). If you have a crop of 30 or 60 times more, that means you are seeing some prayers answered but not all. Satan has stolen some things from you but not everything.

God wants us to have 100 times more. God answers all our prayers when we pray in faith according to His will. But we must keep His Word in our heart in order to receive the answers to our prayers. Jesus had a crop of 100 times more. We can look at His life and learn how to do the same. Keep in mind that if you don't hear God's Word at all, then you are not included in this parable. You have no chance of producing any fruit without hearing God's Word.

Guard Your Heart

How do you know when God's Word has grown in your heart? One way you will know is by how you act when bad things happen. If you are often worried or scared, His Word has not yet grown in your heart. Complaining is also a sign of His Word not yet grown. And if a problem comes and you start speaking words that do not agree with the Bible, then you know His Word has not grown in your heart.

God said, "Above all else, guard your heart. Everything you do comes from it" (Prov. 4:23 NIrV). We must be very careful not to let things in this world steal God's Word from us. Make God most important in your life. When you do, you will find that you act and think differently than most other people in this world. This is a good thing! As believers in Jesus, we are supposed to be different. If you find yourself always doing what is popular or what most other people are doing, this may be a sign that you've let other things crowd out the Word of God and are not guarding your heart. (See Appendix B for more on guarding your heart.)

A Great Storm

After Jesus taught the parable of the sower to a big crowd of people, He said to His disciples, "Let us cross over to the other side" (Mark 4:35 NKJV). Jesus wanted to cross the sea in a boat with His twelve disciples (or followers). After they started to the other side, a huge windstorm came. The waves were so big that the boats were starting to fill with water. His disciples thought everyone was going to die. However, Jesus was asleep on a pillow in the back of the boat. The Bible says:

> His disciples woke Jesus and said, "Teacher, don't you care if we drown?" He got up, rebuked the wind and said to the waves, "Quiet! Be still!"

Then the wind died down and it was completely calm. He said to his disciples, "Why are you so afraid? Do you still have no faith?" (Mark 4:38-40 NIV)

Jesus spoke words before they went out to sea. He said, "Let us cross over to the other side." God always says what He means. He said they will go to the other side. If they would have drowned, they would not have made it to the other side like Jesus said.

The disciples *heard* His words about going to the other side. And they had also just heard His words about the parable of the sower. Then, on the same day, a problem came (the storm). Immediately, Satan tried to steal the words they had just heard (just as the parable of the sower says). How did the disciples respond to the problem? They were worried, they were scared, and they spoke words of unbelief. They talked about drowning instead of the fact that Jesus said they would go to the other side. They let Satan win and steal God's Word.

How did Jesus respond to the problem? He was asleep! He didn't see the problem the same way as the disciples did. He had faith they would make it to the other side. Jesus didn't cry for help. He was not scared or worried. And He used *words* that matched the Word of God to rebuke the storm. He said to the waves, "Quiet! Be still!" He did not let Satan win. He believed and spoke God's Word.

We can also rebuke our own problems using God's Word. If we have God's Word planted in our heart, and we tell Satan to leave us alone, he has no choice but to listen to us. The Bible says, "Therefore submit to God. Resist the devil and he will flee from you" (James 4:7 NKJV).

It is important that we have God's Word planted in our heart and give it time to grow. You can't wait until a problem comes and *then* look in the Bible for something to believe and say. Jesus said Satan "comes only to steal and kill and destroy; I have come that they may have life, and have it to the full" (John 10:10 NIV). We will talk more about this in the next chapter.

✝

READ:
Genesis 3
John 8:31-47

SATAN TWISTS GOD'S WORDS

Memory Verse:
I can do all things through Christ who strengthens me.
Philippians 4:13 (NKJV)

There are a lot of things in life that are designed to protect us from harm. Seatbelts, bicycle helmets, shoes, warm clothes in the winter, and sunscreen are some of those things. Did you know God has an entire set of armor that is used for protection, and He has given it to us? Since it's the same armor that God uses, we know that it must be strong!

In this chapter, we will begin to talk about why we need God's armor for protection. Then, in Chapter 12, we will take a closer look at God's sword and learn how to use it.

The Serpent

God created all things to be perfect. He created Adam and Eve, the first man and woman, and put them in a perfect garden called the Garden of Eden. God told them they could eat from any tree in the garden except for one. This tree was called "the tree of the knowledge of good and evil" (Gen. 2:16-17 NKJV). God told Adam and Eve they would die if they ate from this tree. However, God did not force them to obey. He gave them a choice.

Adam and Eve spent their time in a perfect world, in a perfect garden, with perfect lives. God even came to walk with them in the cool of the day (Gen. 3:8). However, one day a serpent showed up. The Bible said he was more crafty than all the other animals of the field (Gen. 3:1). This means he was clever (or tricky) in a dishonest way.

The serpent went to Eve and began asking her questions. Through his questioning, the serpent started to change Eve's way of thinking. He took a little bit of truth and twisted it into a lie. He was trying to trick her with his words and it worked. She started thinking about what it would be like if she was wise like God. And she saw how good the fruit looked on the tree that she was told not to eat. Eve made a decision based on what she saw and thought instead of what God had said. She decided to eat from the forbidden tree. Then she told Adam to do the same. God did not want anything bad to happen to Adam and Eve. But God cannot lie, and He can only act in a fair way (Num. 23:19). He could not ignore what Adam and Eve did.

When Adam and Eve disobeyed God, sin immediately came. Sin brought death and bad things into the world. Since Adam and Eve, sin is passed down to every person born. Sin makes a person separated from God. The punishment for sin is death (Rom. 6:23). If we die with sin, we will be separated from God forever in hell. This is the reason Jesus came and died for us. He took our punishment and removed the separation between God and people (John 3:16, 1 John 2:2).

The Serpent Acted with Words

The disobedience of Adam and Eve happened because of words. God spoke words to them. He said, "You may eat fruit from any tree in the garden. But you must not eat the fruit from the tree of the knowledge of good and evil. If you do, you will certainly die" (Gen. 2:16-17 NIrV). Adam and Eve heard His words and believed His words for a time. Then Satan (as the serpent) came to steal God's words. Notice Satan didn't come as a lion and try to bite them if they didn't listen. He didn't come as a huge bear and try to scare them. He came as a snake with no threat to bite them. He tried to trick Adam and Eve using his own words. Satan did not force them to disobey God. They were given a choice.

Satan will try to do the same thing to you. He will use words to try to change your way of thinking. He might use another person to speak false words to you. Or he might put thoughts in your mind. He will try to make you think differently, or he will try to make you doubt and lose faith. He will try to make you become discouraged or angry. He will try to put thoughts of worry, fear, or panic in you. He will try to make you question what God really said, and he can even try to make you blame things on God.

Satan said to Eve, "Did God really say, 'You must not eat fruit from any tree in the garden'?" (Gen. 3:1 NIrV). No, God did not say that. He said they could not eat from *only one* tree. But Satan took some of that truth and twisted it into a lie.

Then Satan said to Eve, "You will not die. God knows that if you eat the fruit from that tree, you will learn about good and evil and you will be like God!" (Gen. 3:4-5 NCV). This is another truth twisted into a lie. Adam and Eve *would* know the difference between good and evil when they ate the fruit. In doing so, evil would come into the world and they would know about evil just like they knew about good. However, Satan also lied. He made sin sound like a good thing. He told them eating the fruit would make them be like God, and He made God sound like the liar. However, they did not become like God. And they did die just as God said. They died immediately in their spirit and their bodies also died at a later time.

After Satan spoke these words, Eve started thinking that the fruit looked good. She thought about becoming wise like God (Gen. 3:6). She thought about things she had never thought of before. And it was because she had listened to Satan's words. He had changed her way of thinking.

Satan tries to fight a battle with you in your mind. He wants to tear you away from God. He wants you to disobey God, and he does not want you to believe God's words. Sadly, the Bible says that more people in this world will choose to listen to Satan instead of God (Matt. 7:13-14). The Bible says Satan "was a murderer from the beginning and was against the truth, because there is no truth in him. When he tells a lie, he shows what he is really like, because he is a liar and the father of lies" (John 8:44 NCV).

Believers Have God's Spirit

So what can we do? Should we be afraid of Satan? Not at all! He has no power over you if you do not let him. When you believe in Jesus and are born again, you have God's Spirit inside you (1 Cor. 3:16). This Spirit is the same Spirit that raised Jesus from the dead (Rom. 8:11). His Spirit has all power and all wisdom. The Bible says, "God's Spirit, who is in you, is greater than the devil, who is in the world" (1 John 4:4 NCV).

When Jesus died on the cross, he defeated Satan (Col. 2:15). And one day, Satan will be thrown into hell forever. The Bible says, "And Satan, who tricked them, was thrown into the lake of burning sulfur [hell]...There they will be punished day and night forever and ever" (Rev. 20:10 NCV brackets added). Until then, Satan will run from us if we fight him (James 4:7). And God has given us everything we need to do that. He has given us His sword, and the Holy Spirit will help us use it. In fact, because of Satan, God has given us His *whole* armor. In the next chapter, we will continue to learn about God's armor and His sword.

✝

READ:
Ephesians 6:10-18
Luke 4:1-15

GOD'S WORD IS A SWORD

Memory Verse:
Therefore submit to God. Resist the devil and he will flee from you. James 4:7 (NKJV)

When Jesus was born, the Romans oversaw the land. Roman governors were the leaders of the people, and Roman soldiers made sure people followed the laws. The Roman soldiers were equipped with armor that they used to fight and protect themselves. Their armor included a helmet, belt, a breastplate (that protected their heart), shoes, a shield, and a sword.

The sword was the piece of armor that was used to fight the enemy. The sword was their weapon and the rest of the armor was for protection.

These soldiers received large amounts of training on how to use their sword. They knew that just having a sword on their belt would do no good unless they knew how to use it properly.

In the previous chapter, we learned the reason God has given us His entire armor. In this chapter, we will learn about God's sword, and how we can properly use it.

The Armor of God

Ephesians 6 tells us about the armor of God. God gives us the same armor that He uses; He doesn't just give us part of it. The Bible says, "Put on **all** of God's armor. Then you can remain strong against the devil's evil plans" (Eph. 6:11 NIrV emphasis added). Notice the Bible doesn't say put on God's armor so *He* can fight the devil (Satan) for you. It says put it on so *you* can. God has given you the power, protection, and weapon to stand against Satan. And since it belongs to God, we know that nothing can overpower it (Rom. 8:31).

It is important to understand the meaning of each piece of God's armor. But for now, we are going to focus on His sword. The Bible tells us exactly what God's sword is. It says, "And take...the sword of the Spirit, which is the word of God..." (Eph. 6:17 NKJV).

How Can We Use the Sword?

Remember from chapter six, there are two different Greek words that are used for God's word. *Rhema* is the spoken word, and *logos* is God's written word. In Ephesians 6 when it says the sword is God's word, it is talking about *rhema*. The power of the sword comes from God's written word. But we release the power by *speaking* His written Word. When we speak what the Bible says, we are using the sword of the Spirit. No weapon is more powerful than God's sword.

If you are a follower of Jesus, did you know that you have already used God's sword? You heard God's Word, you believed it, and then you **spoke** it (or prayed) to be saved from sin. The Bible says, "If you declare with your mouth, "Jesus is Lord," and believe in your heart that God raised him from the dead, you will be saved" (Rom. 10:9 NIV). (We discussed this in more detail in Chapter 8.)

Moses and the Rock

The book of Numbers tells about a time that Moses was leading the Israelites (God's chosen people) through the wilderness (Num. 1-20). They were headed to a land God had promised to give them. The Israelites started complaining that they were thirsty. This had happened a time before (Ex. 17:1-7). The first time, God told Moses to *hit* a rock with his staff (his walking stick). Moses hit the rock and water came out, giving the Israelites a drink.

The second time, God told Moses to take his staff and **speak** to the rock. God said the rock would give all the people water to drink. However, Moses was upset with the Israelites. Instead of speaking, he hit the rock twice with his staff. Moses didn't listen to God, but God gave them water out of the rock to drink anyway. God told Moses that, because he didn't speak to the rock as he was told, he would not enter the Promised Land with the Israelites.

We find out later in the Bible that God gave Moses this punishment because the rock was meant to show how things would work in the future (1 Cor. 10:4). The rock represented Jesus and was there to supply their need. The first time, Moses was supposed to *hit* the rock. This is like Jesus being crucified (or dying on a cross). The second time, Moses was supposed to *speak* to the rock. Speaking to the rock was supposed to show that this how you get life out of the rock (or Jesus) *after* He has been crucified.

This example shows us how the Kingdom of God works. God meets our needs as we speak His Word. His written Word is living and powerful, and we release that power by speaking it (Heb. 4:12).

Jesus Uses the Sword of the Spirit

In the book of Revelation, John tells about a vision he had of heaven. He said he saw Jesus with a sharp two-edged sword coming out of His mouth (Rev. 1:16). The sword was in His mouth, not in His hand. This represents Jesus using the sword of the Spirit. Jesus also says in a later verse that He will fight with the sword of His mouth (Rev. 2:16). The Bible says this sword Jesus uses is so powerful it can strike down entire nations (Rev. 19:15). God's sword is the most powerful weapon in the universe, and He has given it to us. It's the same spoken word that was used to create the universe.

Jesus Was Tempted by Satan

After Jesus was baptized in water, He was filled with the Holy Spirit and was led into the wilderness. While He was there, Satan tempted Jesus by speaking words (Luke 3:21-23; 4:1-13). When you are *tempted* or have a *temptation*, it means you have a strong desire to have or do something (especially something that is wrong). Satan tempted Jesus to do things that were wrong. By reading about the temptations of Jesus in the Bible, we can learn more about the sword of the Spirit. Jesus used the sword to fight Satan by speaking words that are in the Bible. Here is an example:

> Then the devil led Jesus up to a high place. In an instant, he showed Jesus all the kingdoms of the world. He said to Jesus, "I will give you all their authority and glory. It has been given to me, and I can give it to anyone I want to. If you worship me, it will all be yours." Jesus answered, "It is written, 'Worship the Lord your God. He is the only one you should serve.'" (Luke 4:5-8 NIrV)

This was really a temptation for Jesus. Even though Jesus was still fully God, He had also become fully human (Phil. 2:7). It took effort for Jesus to say no. Jesus used the sword by speaking words from the book of Deuteronomy (6:13). Out of all the things Jesus could have done, He used the sword against Satan.

We are told of four times that Satan tried to tempt Jesus in the wilderness. Each time, Jesus used the sword. After the fourth time, the Bible says Satan "left Jesus until a better time" (Luke 4:13 NIrV). Satan realized he could not do anything to Jesus because Jesus was swinging His sword! If we resist Satan, he has to flee (James 4:7).

God gives us the same sword that Jesus used. We shouldn't choose our own words to speak to Satan. We must say what is written in God's Word. Satan fled from Jesus and he will also flee from you. But you have to put God's Word in your heart *before* Satan comes, so His Word will have time to grow. Satan wants to steal God's Word from you because Satan knows we will be able to use it as a sword against him later.

Training to Use Your Armor

Just as a soldier spends many hours in training to learn how to use their weapons, so should we. If you are not comfortable using the sword at first, don't give up. Ask God to help you through the Holy Spirit. Reading the Bible and books like this one will help you learn how to use your armor with success. (See Appendix C for more examples on how to use the sword of the Spirit.)

✝

READ:
Ezekiel 28:11-19
Psalm 8
Luke 10:1-20

WHO IS IN CHARGE?

Memory Verse:
He who is in you is greater than he who is in the world.
1 John 4:4 (NKJV)

If someone has authority or dominion, it means they have the right to be in charge. My parents have authority (or are in charge) of me. The president of the United States has authority over the country. God has all authority and power. The Bible says, "The Lord Most High is awesome; He is a great King over all the earth" (Ps. 47:2 NKJV). It aslo says Jesus is the "King of kings and the Lord of lords" (Rev. 19:16 NIV). God has authority and dominion over all His creation. However, the Bible says that God gave dominion to people (Gen. 1:26). He put people in charge of the animals and the earth. The Bible also says

Satan is called the "god of this world" and the "prince of this world" (2 Cor. 4:4; John 14:30 NIrV). It also says some people are under the control of Satan (Eph. 2:2). So, who is really in charge? Let's read more to find out.

Did God Create Satan?

The name Satan means "adversary" which means an enemy. And that is exactly what Satan is: our enemy. God did not create Satan, but He created Lucifer as an angel of God (Is. 14:12). The Bible describes Lucifer as being full of wisdom and beauty. He was covered with every kind of precious stone, and he had a place of authority among the angels (Ez. 28:12-19).

The Bible says Lucifer did nothing wrong from the day he was created until the day evil was found in him (Ez. 28:15 NIV). Like all other created beings, God made Lucifer with the ability to make his own choices. Lucifer fell into pride (Ez. 28:17). This means he thought too highly of himself. He fell in love with his own beauty and wisdom. Lucifer wanted to be equal to or above God (Is. 14:12-14). The Bible says he was filled with violence and sinned. Because Lucifer sinned, God threw him out of heaven (Ez. 28:16). He was no longer an angel of God, and he is now called Satan or the devil.

Where is Satan Now?

The Bible says Satan has come to "steal and kill and destroy" (John 10:10 NIV). Right now, Satan is roaming the earth. The Bible says, "Your enemy the devil is like a roaring lion. He prowls around looking for someone to swallow up" (1 Peter 5:8

NIrV). Satan does what he can to try to destroy you, distract you, lie to you, and take your attention away from God. Satan is called the father of lies (John 8:44). He wants you to listen to his evil lies instead of following God.

Is Satan Really in Charge of This World?

Jesus called Satan the "ruler of this world" (John 14:30 NKJV). Satan is also called a ruler of darkness and the "prince of the power of the air" (Eph. 2:2, 6:12 NKJV). Satan is called a ruler, but does he really have authority?

1. God has final authority.

The Bible says that God is *sovereign*. This means God is all-powerful, He knows all, He is everywhere at once, and His decision is final. He has the highest power and authority. The Bible says, "His Kingdom rules over all" (Ps. 103:19 NKJV). God said to Job, "Everything under heaven is Mine" (Job 41:11 NKJV).

2. God gave dominion over the earth to people.

God has final authority over all creation. However, after God made man, He gave Adam (and all human beings) *dominion* over the earth (Gen. 1:26). This means God gave us control of the entire planet. God created us in His image and likeness. And He made us with the ability to rule over the earth.

The Bible says, "Heaven belongs to the Lord, but he gave the earth to people" (Ps 115:16 NCV). It also says, "You put them in charge of everything you made. You put all things under their control" (Ps. 8:6 NCV). Even though God has final control and He is the highest power, He has made people in charge of the earth.

God is not controlling what we do. God gives us the freewill to make our own choices. Since we can make our own choices, God cannot force us to do anything we do not want to do. Therefore, by God's choice, He does not have complete control over us. This does not mean that we have the same power as God. We are *not* sovereign as God is sovereign, but we have been put in charge of the earth and can make our own choices.

3. People gave their dominion over to Satan.

When Adam and Eve sinned, they gave their dominion over to Satan. Satan had dominion over the earth that was cursed with sin. It was not God's plan or will for this to happen. God did not give dominion to Satan or bring sin into the world. People did. Adam and Eve were not forced to listen to Satan. And Satan was not forced to trick Adam and Eve. God gives everyone a choice, and they all made the wrong choice.

4. Jesus came and took away Satan's dominion.

God did not create the world so Satan could rule over it. He did not create a world full of sin. And He did not create people to be separated from Him. So, God sent His Son to destroy the rule of Satan. When Jesus died on the cross, He took Satan's rule away from him (John 12:31; Gal. 1:4). The Bible says, "But the Son of God came to destroy the devil's work" (1 John 3:8 NIrV).

Jesus took Satan's authority away, but Satan is still allowed to roam the earth in this age. This is why we still must use our sword against him. However, there will be a second time when Jesus will come to earth. He will then take Satan's power away completely, and Satan will be thrown into hell (1 Cor. 15:24-28). Satan will no longer have rule over anyone.

5. Jesus took away Satan's authority and gave it back to people.

When Jesus took Satan's authority away on the cross, Jesus gave it back to those who believe in Him. Jesus said, "I have given you *authority* to trample on snakes and scorpions and to overcome all the power of the enemy; nothing will harm you" (Luke 10:19 NIV emphasis added). Snakes and scorpions are a symbol of Satan and demons (Satan's spiritual helpers). **Jesus gave believers authority over Satan.**

The Bible says, "God's Spirit, who is in you, is greater than the devil, who is in the world (1 John 4:4 NCV). Those who choose to believe and follow Jesus have been given authority to rule over Satan with God's Spirit. We have been given the armor of God, including the sword of the Spirit, for a reason. He has given us the ability to overcome Satan, but we must make the choice to do so.

6. Satan still rules over those who do not believe in Jesus.

Those who do not believe in Jesus are still under Satan's rule (Eph. 2:2). They are said to be like Satan's children (John 8:44, 1 John 3:8). Therefore, this is why Jesus calls Satan the "ruler of this world". When He says, "this world", He is not talking about the created earth. He is referring to all those on the earth who do not believe in Jesus.

So, who is really in charge? God is sovereign and has final control. However, God has given all people the ability to make their own choices. Therefore, God does not control everything we do. Believers have been given authority over Satan. But Satan has rule over those who do not believe in Jesus.

Why Can't God Throw Satan into Hell Right Now?

The Bible does not give us all the answers about Satan. But we do know some things. God has *not* taken Satan out of the world and *forced* people to believe in Jesus. God wants people to love and serve Him voluntarily. He wants it to be their choice. God does not force people to do anything. And He has not left us alone to deal with Satan. Jesus has already defeated Satan on the cross, and He has given us everything we need to overcome him.

God's plan for His people is amazing. God placed a man and a woman, made in His image, on a perfect earth. He did this so they could have a relationship with Him. However, God did not force them to love Him. Satan tempted Adam and Eve and they had a choice. When they didn't choose God, He did not get angry. He did not destroy them. God, acting in love, started His plan of redemption (a plan to save us) and win back His special creation. God sent His only Son to suffer and die a horrible death so we wouldn't have to.

One day, when the time is right, God will have many people who freely love Him. At that point, God will give Satan what he deserves. God will put Satan in hell where he cannot escape for one thousand years (Rev. 20:2-3). With Jesus being in charge, God will show all people what a world without Satan is like. Then Satan will be set free for a time, and he will make one last effort to destroy Jesus and His people. But he will fail. Satan cannot overcome God's power, and he will be totally defeated and sent to hell forever (Rev. 20:7-10).

All people who choose to believe in Jesus will spend forever with God in a perfect heaven with perfect bodies. They will enjoy a city that has streets of gold, gates of pearls, and walls of precious stones. There will be no nighttime, no moon, and no sun because God is the light in heaven (Rev. 21:23). There will be no sin, sickness, fear, sadness, or worry. There will be no more threat of Satan. People will be made kings and queens, live in mansions, and have great rewards and surprises waiting for them. There will be a river, with the clearest water you have ever seen, flowing from the throne of God (Rev. 22:1). The tree of life, the tree God gave Adam and Eve in the beginning, will also be in heaven. And the best part of all, we will see Jesus face to face.

Remember, God and Satan are not equal. Satan is a created being. He does not have the same power as God. He cannot be in all places at once. There are some questions about Satan that cannot be answered in this age. We know he is our enemy, and the Bible tells us to be alert that Satan is here (1 Peter 5:8). It's important to be aware of who he is and what he does, so we can be prepared to stop him. But we shouldn't spend too much time focusing our attention on Satan. He wants you to think that he has more power than what he really does. We should spend time learning about God and enjoying our relationship with Him. No one will get to heaven one day and say, "God, you have acted very unfairly." We will see how good, loving, and fair God really is to all of creation.

✝

MERCY AND GRACE

Memory Verse:
For by grace you have been saved through faith, and that
not of yourselves; it is the gift of God.
Ephesians 2:8 (NKJV)

*We know that God created the world to be perfect and it
was perfect for a time. But sin changed the world. There
are still good things in this world, but there are also
bad. I have heard many people say that bad things are
God's fault. They say God causes or allows bad things to
happen to teach us a lesson. Is this true?*

Good Things Come from God

God doesn't cause bad things to happen to you. But that's
what Satan wants you to think. Why would God say that He

has healed every sickness and then turn around and cause us to be sick? Why would God say He will give us what we need, but then turn around and take some of those things away? The answer is He would not do those things. God doesn't give us something just so He can take it away or destroy it later. Jesus said a kingdom divided against itself cannot stand (Mark 3:24). This means God is either on our side or He's not. He either loves us or He wants to make us miserable. He doesn't do both.

Satan is the thief, liar, and murderer, not God. God gives us life. He not only gives us what we need but more than we need. He not only loves us, but He is love. It is so important to learn who God really is and not have wrong ideas about Him. He is your Father who loves you more than you could ever understand. He would never harm you in any way. And when the time is right, we will join Him in a perfect place that is far better than we could ever imagine.

Sin Changed the World

God designed the world to be perfect. He made us in His image so we could enjoy a relationship with Him and He could bless us. Sin was not part of God's design. However, Adam and Eve made a choice to not listen to God. Their disobedience brought sin into the world (Rom. 5:12). What a horrible choice Adam and Eve made! They were told to leave the perfect garden forever and now lived in a world full of sin. They were separated from the One who loved them most.

God could have been very angry with Adam and Eve, but He didn't give up on them. He could have destroyed Adam and

Eve and started over by making two new people. God hates sin. Sin changed the world, but God still loved His people. He still wanted to have a relationship with them, and they were still His special treasure. God had a plan to get the world back to the way He originally designed it.

God Shows His Mercy and Grace

Imagine what God's voice must have sounded like when He spoke to Adam and Eve and said, "What is this you have done?" (Gen. 3:13 NKJV). He didn't sound angry. "The Lord shows mercy and is kind. He does not become angry quickly, and he has great love" (Ps. 103:8 NCV). He must have sounded sad and hurt.

God couldn't ignore what Adam and Eve did because God can only act fairly. God had already warned them what would happen if they disobeyed. However, God didn't just send them out of the garden and say, "Good luck. You're on your own." God showed His mercy to Adam and Eve right away. He made them clothes to wear, and He promised to send His Son to rescue them (Gen. 3:15, 21). He knew they were embarrassed to be naked and cared about them. He cared how they felt, and He cared about their needs. He cared about them even though they did not deserve it. They had just done something that was going to badly affect the earth until the end of this age. With one choice, they had greatly changed God's perfect creation. But God still loved them. He showed them His grace and mercy. He was still the same God that is loving, forgiving, kind, and patient.

Someone who has never read the Bible before might expect to read about people who have lived a near perfect life. They might expect to read about those who didn't make mistakes, who always did what God asked them to do, and who set great examples for all to follow. There are many great examples in the Bible. However, the Bible is also full of imperfect people.

Adam and Eve disobeyed God. Abraham said his wife was his sister and went to Egypt when he should have stayed put. Jacob tricked his father by putting animal hair on his arms to receive a blessing. Moses didn't listen to God and hit a rock instead of speaking to it. David had a man killed because he wanted the man's wife. Solomon had 700 wives. Jonah tried to run away when God told him to go to Nineveh. Samson made one bad decision after another. When Jesus was arrested, His closest friends left Him and said they didn't know Him. The list goes on and on.

Although each story is different, God reacts the same way. The Bible is full of God's **mercy** and **grace**. The Bible says:

> But because of his great love for us, God, who is rich in mercy, made us alive with Christ even when we were dead in transgressions [sin]... For it is by grace you have been saved, through faith—and this is not from yourselves, it is the gift of God. (Eph. 2:4,5,8 NIV brackets added)

God's grace and mercy means God does things even though we do not deserve it. God showed His mercy and grace to

Adam and Eve in the garden. He helped them and planned to save them even though they did not deserve it. God's mercy and grace is shown throughout the Bible to the imperfect people who put their faith in Him. God still loved and blessed those like Abraham, Moses, David, and Solomon even though they made mistakes and didn't deserve it. In fact, Paul (who wrote over half of the New Testament) used to have Christians killed before he became one himself.

Today, God still gives us His mercy and grace when we choose to put our own faith in Jesus. The Bible says, "But God is faithful and fair. If we confess our sins, he will forgive our sins. He will forgive every wrong thing we have done. He will make us pure" (1 John 1:9 NIrV). Remember, as followers of Jesus, God gives us life and good things even though we do not deserve it.

✝

READ:
Genesis 5
Psalm 148

CREATION AND SCIENCE: PART 1

Memory Verse:
It is better to trust the Lord than to trust people.
Psalm 118:8 (NCV)

At school we studied how the universe began. I thought I already knew the answer. But my science book said nothing about God creating it. I found out that many scientists have come up with ideas that do not include God. Depending on where you go to school, your science book might say a world without God is a fact. Many science classes make it seem like there is no God at all. I even know some people who used to believe in God, but a teacher convinced them that God was not real. Are science and the Bible really that different?

What is Science?

Why do earthquakes happen? How old is the earth? How

does the human heart work? Where do meteors come from? How do animals talk to each other? Science is observing the world and trying to figure out how it works. With science, you can try to answer questions like these and many more. Science includes asking questions, developing ideas, observing, gathering information, and testing. Science has also led to discoveries and inventions such as the telescope, the light bulb, the telephone, and medicines.

Science is Always Changing

People have been studying modern science for around 500 years.[1] During this time, many ideas in science have changed. We now know there are seven continents instead of three. We know the earth is round instead of flat. And we know that the earth revolves around the sun instead of the earth being the center of the universe. These examples were discovered many years ago, but changes in many areas of science are still happening today. *Why?*

Science is based on observation (or looking at something to gain information). But not everything can be observed. For example, we cannot observe things that have happened in the past. Therefore, scientists must make best "guesses" or develop ideas about events that happened long ago. These ideas are tested repeatedly to see if they could be true. In the future, if new information is discovered, these ideas may be changed. There are still many questions and mysteries about the universe that science has not been able to answer.

Scientific Theories and Assumptions

A theory attempts to explain how things work or how they

happen. Simply put, an idea in science can become a theory after repeated testing and when other scientists agree with the idea. A theory is more reliable than a guess, but it can still be proven wrong with better testing or new knowledge.

Some theories are based on things that can be observed (or seen). For example, Isaac Newton was able to observe things falling (like an apple falling from a tree) and made a theory about gravity. Other theories are based on things that cannot be observed such as events that happened in the past. We cannot directly observe the past since we were not there. For example, no one (except God) was present when the universe began. Scientists have made a theory about how it started. But since it was not observed, the theory is based on *assumptions*.

Assumptions can be thought of like "best guesses" or assuming something is true. In other words, scientists use what they *think* they might find if they had been there to see what actually happened. For instance, scientists look at the Grand Canyon *today* and see that rocks are eroding (or wearing away) very slowly. Scientists *assume* the rocks have always eroded at that same slow speed. They use this assumption to say, at this slow speed, it took millions of years for the canyon to form. Therefore, the earth is very old.

However, scientists do not know for sure that the canyon has always eroded at the same speed. They made an assumption because they are not able to observe what happened in the past. They do not ask the question, "What if there was a world-wide flood like the Bible describes?" Flood waters can make rocks break down rapidly. Therefore, with a flood, the Grand Canyon would have been formed very quickly and it really isn't that old after all.

This way of thinking comes from the *principle of uniformity*. This principle is used in science frequently. Many scientists believe what happened in the past is the same as what is happening today. This idea became popular in the 1830's by a scientist who did not believe that God created the universe.[2] Those who believe this idea do not believe there was a world-wide flood that is described in the Bible.

To understand assumptions, look at this simple example.

I see that you have grown one inch in the past year. I will make the assumption that you have always grown one inch each year based on how fast you grew this past year. However, I do not know this for sure. I have made an assumption. Scientists use assumptions to make theories about past events. This can lead to their theories being wrong.

Disagreements in Science

True science cannot completely prove something to be true. Instead, it gives ideas that seem to be true. For example, science cannot tell us how life began, because no one (except God) was there to observe it. Scientists have the theory of evolution, but science cannot prove evolution to be true. True evolution cannot be observed and tested. (Evolution will be explained more in the next chapter.)

Evolution goes against what the Bible says. This is one reason science causes many people to disagree. Not all scientists believe the same thing. Two scientists can look at the same evidence and come up with two completely different ideas. Why does this happen? It is partly to do with what the scientist *already* believes. For instance, if a scientist does not believe in God, his answers will likely be different than a scientist who does believe in God. *Why*?

Let's say there is a person who has made up their mind, without a doubt, that God is not real. This person will think about life differently. If he sees an amazing animal, he won't say, "Look at the amazing creature that God made!" Instead, he might say, "I wonder how that creature got here and learned to do those things?" Someone with this view refuses to even accept the possibility that God is real. Therefore, they look at questions in science and try to come up with answers that do not include God. Scientists who believe in God and the Bible will usually have much different ideas than a scientist who does not believe in God.

Science in Public Schools

Over the years, public schools have changed in many ways. Today, the Bible and prayer are not allowed in public school. Different ideas, that don't include God, are being taught to students. Many people say that education and religion should be separated.

Schools haven't always been this way. Hundreds of years ago, students read the Bible aloud during class. The alphabet was taught by using names in the Bible (such as A is for Adam). Students were taught to read and learn Bible verses at the same time. Textbooks (also called primers) referred to stories in the Bible. They included the Lord's prayer (Matt. 6:9-13), the ten commandments (Ex. 20:1-18), and the names and order of the books in the Bible.

Today, science without God is not only found in schools but also throughout books, television, movies, and the internet. The ideas of how life began without God are being presented as if they are true, and we are surrounded by them. Satan can even use a school system to try to change your way of thinking.

The Age of the Earth

How old is the earth? If you open a school textbook or search the internet, you will likely see an answer of about 4.5 billion years. Most people who believe this do not believe that God created the universe.

During the 1700's, some scientists started choosing to reject God as our Creator.[3] Instead, they worked on developing ideas in science that did not include God. Today, there are two main beliefs on the age of the earth: it is either about 4.5 billion years old or around 6,000 years old.

The Bible says the beginning of the universe was on day one of creation. The first man, Adam, was made on day six. However, the Bible does not tell us when these days of creation were. Instead, it tells us when people were born, had children, and died.

For example, the Bible says Adam lived to be 930 years old (Gen. 5:8). He had a son when he was 530 (Gen. 5:3). Adam's son, Seth, had a son when he was 105 years old (Gen. 5:6).

Seth had sons and so on. The total years that people lived (as recorded in the Bible) can be added to find an estimate of how old the earth is.

It is commonly estimated that there were 4,000 years between Adam and Jesus's birth. The number of years between Jesus's birth and now can be seen on our calendar. For instance, if it is the year 2015, then it has been about 2,015 years since Jesus was born. Add these numbers and you get approximately 6,000 years.

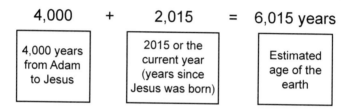

4,000	+	2,015	=	6,015 years
4,000 years from Adam to Jesus		2015 or the current year (years since Jesus was born)		Estimated age of the earth

Some people try to say that one day of creation was much longer than a 24-hour day. They might use the verse in the Bible that says, "with the Lord one day is as a thousand years, and a thousand years as one day" (2 Peter 3:8 NKJV). However, this verse was not talking about creation. It is talking about Jesus's second coming.

God made time and seasons for us. We have the day to work and night to rest (originally working six days and resting on the seventh). In Genesis, it describes the days of creation beginning and ending with night and day (as in a 24-hour day). People who try to say creation took thousands of years are trying to make the Bible match the rest of the unbelieving world who say the earth is very old. The Bible tells us that the earth was made in six days.

✝

CREATION AND SCIENCE: PART 2

Memory Verse:
In the beginning God created the heavens and earth.
Genesis 1:1 (NKJV)

The Big Bang Theory

The "big bang" is an idea in science about how the universe began. The theory says the universe started nearly 14 billion years ago. It started as a tiny, hot point called a *singularity*. You can think of this point to be like a tiny bubble that was much smaller than the point of pencil. The theory says our entire universe was inside this point. However, believers in the big bang say they have no idea where this point came from.

The theory says that one day, this point suddenly exploded. In a fraction of a second, the tiny point grew in size. It continued to grow and things started changing. Stars, planets, and galaxies were eventually formed out of nothing.

After the earth finally cooled, an organism (or a living thing) with a single cell was somehow formed. (To compare, there are *trillions* of cells in one human body.) More organisms were eventually formed; all being so small that you couldn't see them with your eyes. Many scientists say this was the start of life on earth. However, they cannot explain how the organisms got there. Scientists say there was nothing and then, all at once, there was something. They claim it happened randomly (or by accident).

Scientists do not have proof that the big bang happened. It is an idea that scientists try to say is fact. The big bang is based on assumptions. No one was there in the beginning to observe what happened except God. The Bible says God created the universe in six days by speaking words. He spoke it and it happened.

Evolution

The theory of evolution is an idea that tells what happened to the organism (or a tiny speck of life) that appeared after the "explosion". In the 1800's, a man named Charles Darwin made the idea of evolution popular. Simply put, the theory of evolution says that one kind of creature slowly changes into another kind that is more complex (or advanced).

For example, evolution says the tiny specks that showed up after the explosion slowly changed into things like plants and worms. The worms changed into creatures such as jellyfish and crabs. From these creatures, animals with backbones were later formed like fish. Eventually, the sea creatures changed into land animals. The land animals (like chimpanzees) eventually changed into humans. Evolutionists say this took billions of years to happen.

The theory says one of the main ways evolution (or the

changes) happens is by *natural selection*. Let's look at an example of what natural selection is.

Long ago there were black rabbits and white rabbits that lived in a snowy area. The white rabbits were able to hide and blend into the snow. Therefore, they could hide from predators and avoid being killed. The black rabbits, however, could not hide as well and were killed more easily. Since more white rabbits survived, they had more white bunnies. The black rabbits were killed and had very few black bunnies. Eventually, all that were left in the snowy area were the white rabbits. The white rabbits and black rabbits "evolved" (or changed) into being only white rabbits. This is an example of natural selection.

Evolutionists say that not only can small changes (such as color) happen with natural selection, but big changes can happen too (after millions of years). The theory also says that humans have evolved from animals. Evolutionists claim that apes or monkeys (perhaps chimpanzees) slowly changed into humans. Chimps cannot talk or do things that humans can. However, during a long period of time, evolutionists say chimps slowly became smarter. Their looks and body parts changed. They learned to talk, have jobs, build houses, and do many other things. The theory of evolution says that people, along with all other living things, originally came from bacteria that appeared from nothing. After billions of years, we slowly evolved into talking, walking, intelligent human beings.

This, of course, is not what the Bible says. Those who believe in evolution cannot provide proof that it is true. Science involves being able to *observe* and *test* ideas. Evolution and the big bang cannot be observed or tested. The "proof" evolutionists have is based on assumptions or best guesses.

Natural selection is real. And some people think that since it is real, evolution must also be real. (Remember, Satan takes a little truth and mixes it with a lie to try to change your way of thinking.) However, natural selection does *not* work the way evolution claims.

God created all living things with DNA. DNA has information about how a living thing will look and function. For example, DNA determines your hair color, height, and how your lungs work. In order for evolution to be true, *more* information would need to be added to a creature's DNA. To go along with evolution, this new information would be required so the creature could have new abilities and features. For example, a chimp would need new information in their DNA so it could grow taller and learn to speak. However, natural selection works just the opposite. It *selects* from DNA the creature already has. Natural selection *cannot* make new information.

No one can show that natural selection makes one creature turn into another. If a bird's beak changes its shape over time so it can more easily get food, it is not evidence of evolution. The bird is still a bird. Yet many scientists still say that evolution by natural selection is the reason we are here today.

Evolutionists have come up with additional ideas such as mutations that supposedly help creatures evolve or change. But mutations do *not* improve living things or make them more advanced as the theory of evolution claims. Mutations are usually harmful or cause no change.

God gave living things the ability to adapt to their environment so they can survive. In other words, creatures can change in *small* ways that will help them survive. And new *species* of animals can be made such as a new breed of dog. But it is still a dog. A new *kind* of living thing (such as a monkey changing into a man) is not possible. God created all living things in the six days of creation.

The Fossil Record

Fossils are the leftovers of dead animals and plants that have been buried in layers of rock in the earth. Not everything that dies turns into a fossil. Many animals that die are eaten by other animals, or they decay (or rot) until there is nothing left. You may have seen this happening when you drive by a dead animal on the side of the road.

Special conditions must happen for fossils to be made. For instance, if a dead animal is buried very quickly, the bones (and sometimes other things) are saved from being destroyed. The remains of these dead creatures will be formed into a fossil.

Scientists study fossils to try to learn more about the Earth's past. But scientists have different views about the fossil record (or the total number of fossils found). Those who believe in evolution say that the dead plants and animals found in the bottom layers of rock lived millions of years before the ones found in the top layers. And some say that when they find fossils, the simplest creatures are in the "older" bottom layers of rock. In other words, evolutionists claim the fossil record shows the order in which the creatures changed into another creature. They say the fossil record provides proof that evolution is true.

However, many scientists ignore or make excuses when fossils have been found in the wrong order. In other words, scientist have found "older" fossils buried on top of "younger"

fossils. This is exactly opposite of the evolutionary theory.

In addition, scientists have made a scale called a *geological column*. This scale in divided into different periods of time. When they find a fossil, scientists can supposedly look at the scale and tell about how old the fossil should be. If they find a certain type of dinosaur, for example, the scale will tell them how many millions of years old it is.

The problem with the scale (or geological column) is that it has never been completely observed in real life. It is based on assumptions and cannot be proven. It is simply a guess. However, many scientists still use it as fact.

Most scientists who believe that God is our Creator also believe that God flooded the entire earth a little more than 4,000 years ago. The flood explains why there are so many fossils found around the world. With the flood in mind, the fossil record does not show the order in which the animals *lived*. It shows the order in which they were *buried*. The animals on the bottom layers were buried before animals on the top layers.

The fossil record does *not* prove that one living thing changed into another living thing. In addition, the large amount of time that the evolutionists say it took to make these layers also *cannot* be proven. If you consider a world-wide flood, the fossils were buried very quickly. The fossil record as used by most scientists is based on assumptions and does *not* prove that evolution is true.[1]

Radiometric Dating

Many parts of the earth are made of *igneous* rocks. Igneous rocks are made from magma inside the earth or lava from volcanoes. Scientists have figured a way to determine the age of fossils by finding the age of these nearby rocks. Scientists measure the *radioactive elements* found inside the igneous rocks. This type of element gives off energy and starts to decay (or break down) over time.

Scientists know the *half-life* of these elements. The half-life is the time it takes for half of the element to decay.[2] Scientists complete an equation (or math problem) to find the age of the rock. Then they assume the fossil found near the rock is also the same age.

However, to do the math, scientists must know how much of the element was in the rock when it was first made. There is no way to know for sure how much element the rock started with because no one was there to measure it. Therefore, the scientists must make best guesses to come up with a starting number to finish their equation. Their guess is based on what they already believe about the earth being extremely old. Therefore, they are using assumptions of an "old" earth to make more assumptions about "old" rocks. This is how they say fossils such as dinosaur bones are millions of years old. It is based on assumptions and cannot be proven.

What Does the Bible Say?

The very first verse in the Bible says, "In the beginning God created the heavens and the earth" (Gen. 1:1 NKJV). If you believe this verse to be true, then you know that the theories in science about how life began are false. The ideas of evolution and the big bang have become very popular with people who do not believe in God. And it has forced God out of science and our schools.

Humans are the only living beings that God created in His image (Gen. 1:26). He created each living thing according to their kind (Gen. 1:24). This means dogs can only have puppies. Cats can only have kittens. Chickens can only have chicks. There may be different breeds of dogs and cats (like a Poodle, Bulldog, Siamese, or Persian). But they are still dogs and cats. One living thing cannot turn into another living thing, even if you give it millions of years to happen.

God used His words to create all living things (Gen. 1). He spoke it and it was done. Therefore, the universe *did* have a beginning. But it wasn't by an explosion of a tiny point billions of year ago. God says the earth was created in six days. And based on the history of the Bible, that was only about 6,000 years ago. Christians do not have to make "best guesses". The Bible clearly tells us how the universe was made. Everyone is given a choice to believe the Word of God or the words of scientists.

Some evolutionists claim that it takes faith to believe in God, not evidence. It does take faith to believe in God. But it also takes faith to believe in evolution and the big bang. No one has seen evolution happen. No one can prove that it happened. Therefore, it takes faith to believe in evolution. But it is *not* faith in the Creator of the universe. It is faith in the ideas of imperfect human beings. The Bible says, "It is better to trust the Lord than to trust people" (Ps. 118:8 NCV). God does give everyone a choice. But no matter what you choose, God's Word is still truth.

†

READ:
Job 40
Job 41

CREATION AND SCIENCE: PART 3

Memory Verse:
Then God said, "Let the earth be filled with animals, each producing more of its kind. Genesis 1:24 (NCV)

I have always loved learning about dinosaurs. My favorite is the triceratops. But thinking about dinosaurs and the Bible has always been a little confusing. Most information about dinosaurs says they lived millions of years ago. And I haven't found them anywhere in the Bible. How can this be?

Dinosaurs

Most people have seen pictures of dinosaurs in movies and books. Even young children can see them on cartoons and play with their favorite dinosaur toy. Some scientists say that dinosaurs died over 60 *million* years ago. They also say they lived *before* humans lived. For most people, it is hard to imagine dinosaurs and humans living together. Dinosaur fossils have been found all over the world and are still being found today. Everyone agrees that dinosaurs were once alive. However, not everyone agrees on how they got here and when they were alive. Let's review some questions many people have.

1. How long ago were the dinosaurs alive?

The Bible says the earth is only about 6,000 years old. Therefore, dinosaurs did *not* live millions of years ago. Instead, they lived a few thousand years ago.

2. How do scientists find the age of a dinosaur fossil?

The age of dinosaur fossils is usually found by using radiometric dating. This method is explained in chapter 16. To find the age, scientists look at specific elements inside igneous rocks that are found near the fossils. They complete an equation (or math problem) that gives them an estimated age. However, to be able to do the equation correctly, scientists need to know how much of a specific element was in the rock when it was first formed. Scientists do not know that amount because they were not there to measure it when the rock was first made. Therefore, scientists must make a best guess on what the amount was. Their guess (or assumption) is based on the scientist already believing that the earth is millions of years old. To put it simply, the age of dinosaur fossils given by most scientists is a best guess.

3. Did dinosaurs live at the same time as people?

God created dinosaurs on the sixth day of creation. The Bible says, "God made every kind of wild animal. He made every kind of creature that moves along the ground. And God saw that it was good" (Gen. 1:25 NIrV). This would include dinosaurs. Also on the sixth day, "God created man in His own image...male and female He created them" (Gen. 1:27 NKJV). Humans and dinosaurs were created on the same day. Therefore, according to the Bible, humans *did* live at the same time as dinosaurs.

4. Were dinosaurs on Noah's ark?

The Bible says during the time of Noah, people had become so evil that God decided to flood the whole earth. Everything they did and everything they thought about was evil. Noah was the only one that was different. God saved Noah, Noah's family, and two of every kind of animal from being killed in the flood. They were safe in an ark (a large boat) that God told Noah to build (Gen. 6, 7).

Does this mean dinosaurs were on the ark with Noah? Since the Bible tells us that dinosaurs were living at the same time as people, the answer is *yes*. The ark was about 450 to 500 feet long. This is about the size of one and a half football fields. Although there are many kinds of *species* of dinosaur fossils that have been found, there are not quite as many *kinds*. Especially if the dinosaurs were young, there would have been enough room on the ark for two of each kind.

5. Does the Bible say anything about dinosaurs?

The word *dinosaur* was not invented until 1841.[1] Therefore, you will not find the word dinosaur in the Bible because the

Bible was written long before the word was invented. However, the Bible does describe some very interesting creatures. Look at what God said to Job about a creature called *Behemoth* (Job 40:15-17 NIrV):

> Look at Behemoth. It is a huge animal. I made both of you. It eats grass like an ox. Look at the strength it has in its hips! What power it has in the muscles of its stomach! Its tail sways back and forth like a cedar tree...

The study notes in most bibles say that Behemoth might have been a hippopotamus or an elephant. What do you think? Look at the picture below. Which one has a tail like a tree?

Dinosaurs and Dragons

There are ancient stories from all over the world about dragons. People say they were huge creatures that looked similar to dinosaurs. Some even say they breathed fire. Long ago, there were many pictures of these dragons (or dinosaur-like creatures) that were drawn on cave walls, pottery, and stone. These old drawings can be found throughout the world. We have no way of knowing for sure if the stories are real. But why are there so many of them? Where did so many people get an idea for such a creature? How did they all know what dinosaurs looked like before dinosaur fossils were discovered? There were no movies, computers or books that showed them what dinosaurs looked like. Was it because they had seen a real dinosaur?

Did you know that there is a creature in the Bible that breathed fire? When God described Leviathan, He said, "Smoke pours out of its nose, as if coming from a large pot over a hot fire. Its breath sets coals on fire, and flames come out of its mouth" (Job 41:20-21 NCV). Could this have been some sort of a dinosaur-like creature?

The King James Version talks about "dragons" in other parts of the Bible. For example, in Jeremiah, it talks about "a dwellingplace for dragons" (Jer. 51:37 KJV). The original Hebrew word for dragon in this verse is *tanniyn*. The meaning of this word is a "marine or land monster".[2] This word is used 28 times in the Bible and it is sometimes called a dragon, serpent, whale, and sea monster. (See Malachi 1:3, Psalm 74:13, Isaiah 27:1, 43:20; Jeremiah 14:6 in the King James Version.)

Since the word dinosaur was not used when the Bible was written, we cannot know for sure what these creatures were. However, if you believe in the Bible, you know that it says about 6,000 years ago God created the earth in six days. Dinosaurs did *not* live millions of years ago. What happened to the dinosaurs? God is the only One that knows for sure.

✝

NO ONE HAS AN EXCUSE

Memory Verse:
But since the beginning of the world those things have
been easy to understand by what God has made.
Romans 1:20 (NCV)

*I know a man named Jim. He was late to work all the
time. His boss told him if he was late one more time he
would be fired.*

*One morning, Jim woke up late. He got ready for work
quickly but still did not make it on time. Jim had an excuse
for being late. He had slept too long that morning.*

*Jim apologized. He told his boss he tried to make it on
time, but he had overslept. But his boss still had to fire
him for being late again. Jim's excuse did not matter. He
knew he could not be late anymore.*

No One Has an Excuse

God says that people cannot make an excuse for not believing He is real. Everyone, no matter where they live, can look at things that God has made. They can see that there must be a powerful, wise Creator that has made it all. They cannot make an excuse. In the book of Romans, it says:

> God's anger is shown from heaven against all the evil and wrong things people do. By their own evil lives they hide the truth. God shows his anger because some knowledge of him has been made clear to them. Yes, God has shown himself to them. There are things about him that people cannot see - his eternal power and all the things that make him God. But since the beginning of the world those things have been easy to understand by what God has made. So people have no excuse for the bad things they do. They knew God, but they did not give glory to God or thank him. Their thinking became useless. Their foolish minds were filled with darkness. They said they were wise, but they became fools (Rom. 1:18-22 NCV).

Each person can look up at the sky and see there are too many stars to count. Others can see majestic mountains, mysterious caves, enormous oceans, large waterfalls, deep canyons, and unique rainforests. We can see and read about all the amazing animals. And each of us can see a sunrise and sunset each day. We can look at our own body and see how unique and special we were made. God has made it clear to all people that He is real. This earth, and all that is on it, would not be here if God did not exist. No one has an excuse. Not even a person on an island all by themselves.

It does not matter what country you live in, the family you belong to, what type of house you have, the clothes you wear, or whether you are rich or poor. God has put something inside each person to help them see that He exists. For a person to say that God is not real, means they have ignored what God has placed within them. God gives us all a choice, and many people have chosen not to believe.

It is important to be aware that, as a Christian, you will meet many people who disagree with you. Do not let these disagreements make you question what the Bible says. Just as Satan did to Eve in the garden, he will try to use many avenues (such as science) to change your way of thinking. But remember, God and Satan are not equal. We must be aware of Satan's schemes, but there is no reason to be afraid. When you believe in Jesus, the same spirit that raised Jesus from the dead is inside of you (Rom. 8:11). Wherever you are God is there. He is always with you, and He loves you more than you can understand. He will always be there and is ready to speak to you, bless you, protect you, guide you, and provide you with everything you need.

You Have a Choice

Have you ever heard of Albert Einstein? He was a famous scientist who made many new discoveries and was called a genius. As a scientist, he studied many parts of the universe and learned some amazing things about it. He discovered that people could not understand many things about this world. Einstein was so amazed that he was sure there had to be a God who created it all. However, he thought it was not possible to have a personal relationship with God. And he refused to believe in Jesus. He thought the Bible was full of fairytales.[1]

Like everyone else, Einstein had a choice. He had a choice to believe in God. And He also had a choice to believe in Jesus. Jesus said, "I am the way, the truth, and the life. No one comes to the Father except through Me" (John 14:6 NKJV). Looking at what God has made is one way we can learn about Him. We can see His power and wisdom and understanding. We should continue to search for these things like we would search for a hidden treasure. "Then you will find out how to know God" (Prov. 2:5 NIrV). But remember, the only way to receive God's gift of salvation is by believing in His Son, Jesus Christ. We will learn much more about Jesus in the second book of the *Hidden Treasure Quest* series.

†

APPENDIX A
TIPS FOR UNDERSTANDING THE BIBLE

1. The Bible is not like a regular book. You do not have to read it in order. If one book in the Bible is too hard to understand, move on to another and come back to that one later.

2. If you come to a verse that you want to understand better, stop and read it slowly. Read it aloud to yourself many times and focus on what you are reading. This is sometimes called meditating on God's Word. You may notice that the Holy Spirit will help you better understand the verse after doing this.

3. Use a bible dictionary. They are helpful to understand difficult words you may find in the Bible.

4. Jesus is the only perfect person who has ever lived. When you start reading the Bible, don't be surprised when you read about "good" people who made mistakes. For example, the Bible says that David was a man after God's own heart (1 Sam. 13:14). However, David did many things wrong. That doesn't mean David's mistakes were okay. And it doesn't mean God approved of them. God uses imperfect people to do great things. He can't wait for a perfect person to come along because there are none. Jesus is the only perfect person to ever live. We can read the Bible and learn from others' mistakes. And we can learn more about God by reading how He reacted to those mistakes.

5. The Bible is divided into two sections: the *Old Testament* and the *New Testament.* Another word for testament is *covenant.* A covenant is like a very serious promise. The Old Testament tells about the times of the Old Covenant. Those times were much different than they are today. You will read about rules and punishments that may seem confusing. However, there was a reason for the Old Covenant. The purpose was to show each person that they could not be good enough on their own. They need Jesus to save them from their sin. When Jesus died on the cross, the New Covenant started. The New Covenant is still what all believers are under today. It is a better covenant with better promises. However, it is still important that we read the Old Testament. There are many things we need to learn from it. But it's important to not let the Old Covenant be confusing.

6. Be careful what you read. The internet has a lot of helpful information. However, it also has some very bad information. Anyone that knows how can make a website. There is a lot of information on the internet that claims to be explaining the Bible when it really is not. This is the same for other published books. As you learn more of what is in the Bible, you will be able to tell which are good resources to use.

7. Don't give up. The *Hidden Treasure Quest* series is designed to help you understand what is in the Bible and help you know God in a close, personal way. As you read the Bible, the Holy Spirit will help you understand what you are reading.

APPENDIX B
WAYS TO GUARD YOUR HEART

1. **Be careful what you say.** Don't say things that are opposite of what God's Word says. Do not lie or say hurtful things. Don't argue with others and say things you will be sorry for later. Don't speak words of unbelief.

2. **Meditate on the right words.** If you find a verse in the Bible that you want to happen in your life, speak it repeatedly. Think about it often. Memorize it and study it. It will enter your heart and produce fruit if you guard your heart and keep it (Joshua 1:8).

3. **Don't listen to evil talk.** You should not *listen* to words that are not good for you to say (even if you are not the one saying them). This includes things you hear on television or in songs. These words will get into your heart and crowd out God's Word. You will find yourself speaking or thinking about those words and then eventually doing them. Your body follows your words (James 3:2-5).

4. **Be careful what you see.** Your eyes are another way bad things enter your heart and crowd out God's Word. This includes being around the wrong people, seeing wrong things on television or the internet, and reading the wrong books or magazines. Keep your eyes focused on God and godly things. Peter walked on water with Jesus. But when he took his eyes off Jesus and looked at the storm, he started

to sink. We should pay attention to God instead of always thinking about things in this world (Matt. 14:22-33). Faith and good things come from God, not from the world.

5. **Be careful to make right choices.** If you could see Jesus sitting next to you, would He like what you are doing? God's Word helps us make the right choices. But we must take time to read the Bible and develop a relationship with God so we can hear what He is telling us to do. If being around something or someone makes us want to do something bad (or even think about it), we should not even go near that thing or person. "Don't turn to the right or left. Keep your feet from the path of evil" (Prov. 4:27 NIrV).

6. **Think carefully.** In order for you to do something, you first must think about doing it. If you keep thinking about bad things, you'll end up doing bad things. Controlling what you think about is not always easy and it will take practice. Satan uses your thoughts to trick you. Speak God's Word and remind yourself of what they say. As you remind yourself, you might need to say things like: *I know God has answered my prayers. I know God's words are growing inside me right now. I know I am forgiven of my sin. I know God has a plan for my life. I know God loves me and wants only good things for me. I choose to make the right choices and listen to God instead of other people. I know God has healed me. I am not going to worry because God gives me all things I need.* Preach God's Word to yourself, especially when you need help controlling your thoughts.

APPENDIX C

MORE WAYS TO USE THE SWORD OF THE SPIRIT

We Use the Sword by Speaking God's Word

1. **Anger.** If you struggle with getting angry, you can use the sword. Anger is not from God. Put God's Word in your heart about anger. Then speak it when you feel yourself getting angry. For example, read and memorize James 1:19. Then use the sword by saying, "I am quick to listen, slow to speak and slow to get angry."

2. **Fear.** Hebrews 13:6 says, "The Lord *is* my helper; I will not fear" (NKJV). Read and memorize this, getting it into your heart. Then if you find yourself feeling afraid, say, "God is my helper, I will not fear."

3. **Confidence.** In 2 Corinthians 5:21 it says, "God made him who had no sin to be sin for us, so that in him we might become the righteousness of God" (NIV). Read and memorize this verse, getting it into your heart. Then if Satan tries to make you think you are not good enough or you are a bad person, say to him, "Satan, get away from me. I am the righteousness of God."

4. **Worry.** In Philippians 4:19 it says, "And my God shall supply all your need according to His riches in glory by Christ Jesus" (NKJV). If Satan tries to make you worry about money, clothing, food, or other needs you can say,

"Satan, get away from me. My God will supply all my needs."

There are many other examples we could use. You can use any verse in the Bible as a sword. However, the verse should tell Satan He is wrong. For example, let's say Satan tries to tell you that God is not listening to you. Would it help to use the sword by saying, "Noah built the ark"? Instead, you might say, "God's ears are open to the prayers of the righteous", therefore, I know He has heard me (1 Peter 3:12). When you use the sword, use God's Word to tell Satan he is wrong.

Use God's Word When You Pray

We should also use the sword when we pray. If you have a need, find out what the Bible says about it. Put that word into your heart and protect it. Then when you pray, start by saying what God said in His Word. For example:

- God, Your Word says if anyone lacks wisdom they should ask for it and it will be given to them. So, I ask for wisdom in this situation. (James 1:5)

- Father, Your Word says You will supply all my need. So, I ask You for my needs to be met in this situation. (Phil. 4:19)

- God, Your Word says that I will be blessed when I come in and blessed when I go out. So, I ask You to bless me on the trip I am taking today. (Deut. 28:6)

When praying or speaking God's Word, it is ok to put yourself into the verse. For example, the Bible says, "And my

God shall supply all your need..." (Phil 4:19 NKJV). When speaking this verse, you can say "*my* need" instead of "*your* need".

Remember, the Bible says, "Submit to God. Resist the devil and he will flee from you" (James 4:7 NIV). Satan has to flee when you use God's sword. He will come back and try to trick you at a later time, but you'll be ready with God's armor. As you read scripture, make an effort to put it into your heart. Memorize it and protect it. It will grow, produce fruit, and you'll have it ready to use when you need it.

MEMORY VERSES

This is a master list of the memory verses found at the start of each chapter. This list also includes additional verses that do not appear in the chapter headings. For a printable version of this list, visit: www.hideandseekministries.com.

☐ CHAPTER ONE

Memory Verse	Additional Memory Verses	
So God created man in His own image. Genesis 1:27 (NKJV)	If you abide in My word, you are My disciples indeed. John 8:31 (NKJV)	Therefore go and make disciples of all nations. Matthew 28:19 (NIV)

☐ CHAPTER TWO

Memory Verse	Additional Memory Verses	
For we live by faith, not by sight. 2 Corinthians 5:7 (NIV)	So he gave us new life because of what Christ has done. He gave us life even when we were dead in sin. Ephesians 2:5 (NIrV)	The Spirit of God who raised Jesus from the dead is living in you. Romans 8:11 (NIrV)

☐ CHAPTER THREE

Memory Verse	Additional Memory Verses	
In the beginning was the Word, and the Word was with God and the Word was God. John 1:1 (NKJV)	Jesus Christ is the same yesterday, today, and forever. Hebrews 13:8 (NKJV)	Before you created the whole world and the mountains were made, from the beginning to the end you are God. Psalm 90:2 (NIrV)

☐ CHAPTER FOUR

Memory Verse	Additional Memory Verses	
The Lord made the earth by His power. He used his wisdom to build the world and his understanding to stretch out the skies. Jeremiah 51:15 (NCV)	Meditate on it day and night, so that you may be careful to do everything written in it. Joshua 1:8 (NIV)	If any of you needs wisdom, you should ask God for it. He will give it to you. God gives freely to everyone and doesn't find fault. James 1:5 (NIrV)

☐ CHAPTER FIVE

Memory Verse	Additional Memory Verses	
The heavens tell about the glory of God. The skies show that his hands created them. Psalm 19:1 (NIrV)	For all have sinned and fall short of the glory of God. Romans 3:23 (NIV)	Set your minds on things above, not on earthly things. Colossians 3:2 (NIV)

☐ CHAPTER SIX

Memory Verse	Additional Memory Verses	
For the word of God is living and powerful, and sharper than any two-edged sword. Hebrews 4:12 (NKJV)	By faith we understand that the universe was formed at God's command. Hebrews 11:3 (NIV)	All Scripture is God-breathed. 2 Timothy 3:16 (NIV)

☐ CHAPTER SEVEN

Memory Verse	Additional Memory Verses	
Faith comes by hearing, and hearing by the word of God. Romans 10:17 (NKJV)	And you will seek Me and find Me, when you search for Me with all your heart. Jeremiah 29:13 (NKJV)	Trust in the Lord with all your heart, and lean not on your own understanding. Proverbs 3:5 (NKJV)

☐ CHAPTER EIGHT

Memory Verse	Additional Memory Verses	
If you declare with your mouth, "Jesus is Lord," and believe in your heart that God raised him from the dead, you will be saved. Romans 10:9 (NIV)	For God so loved the world that he gave his one and only Son, that whoever believes in him shall not perish but have eternal life. John 3:16 (NIV)	God made him who had no sin to be sin for us, so that in him we might become the righteousness of God. 2 Corinthians 5:21 (NIV)

☐ CHAPTER NINE

Memory Verse	Additional Memory Verses	
Your tongue has the power of life and death. Proverbs 18:21 (NIrV)	If you remain in me and my words remain in you, ask whatever you want, and it will be done for you. John 15:7 (NIrV)	The mouth speaks the things that are in the heart. Matthew 12:34 (NCV)

☐ CHAPTER TEN

Memory Verse	Additional Memory Verses	
Above everything else, guard your heart. Everything you do comes from it. Proverbs 4:23 (NIrV)	The thief comes only to steal and kill and destroy; I have come that they may have life, and have it to the full. John 10:10 (NIV)	Good people think before they answer. Proverbs 15:28 (NCV)

☐ CHAPTER ELEVEN

Memory Verse	Additional Memory Verses	
I can do all things through Christ who strengthens me. Philippians 4:13 (NKJV)	Be strong and brave. Don't be afraid of them and don't be frightened, because the Lord your God will go with you. He will not leave you or forget you. Deuteronomy 31:6 (NCV)	God did not give us a spirit that makes us afraid but a spirit of power and love and self-control. 2 Timothy 1:7 (NCV)

☐ CHAPTER TWELVE

Memory Verse	Additional Memory Verses	
Therefore submit to God. Resist the devil and he will flee from you. James 4:7 (NKJV)	Put on the full armor of God, so that you can take your stand against the devil's schemes. Ephesians 6:11 (NIV)	The Lord is my helper; I will not fear. Hebrews 13:6 (NKJV)

☐ CHAPTER THIRTEEN

Memory Verse	Additional Memory Verses	
He who is in you is greater than he who is in the world. 1 John 4:4 (NKJV)	The Lord Most High is awesome; He is a great King over all the earth. Psalm 47:2 (NKJV)	I have given you authority to trample on snakes and scorpions and to overcome all the power of the enemy; nothing will harm you. Luke 10:19 (NIV)

☐ CHAPTER FOURTEEN

Memory Verse	Additional Memory Verses	
For by grace you have been saved through faith, and that not of yourselves; it is the gift of God. Ephesians 2:8 (NKJV)	For the Lord is good and his love endures forever; his faithfulness continues through all generations. Psalm 100:5 (NIV)	You, Lord, are forgiving and good, abounding in love to all who call to you. Psalm 86:5 (NIV)

☐ CHAPTER FIFTEEN

Memory Verse	Additional Memory Verses	
It is better to trust the Lord than to trust people. Psalm 118:8 (NCV)	Be sure that no one leads you away with false and empty teaching that is only human. Colossians 2:8 (NCV)	Get wisdom, get understanding; do not forget my words or turn away from them. Proverbs 4:5 (NIV)

☐ CHAPTER SIXTEEN

Memory Verse	Additional Memory Verses	
In the beginning God created the heavens and earth. Genesis 1:1 (NKJV)	Is anything too hard for the LORD? Genesis 18:14 (NIV)	Do not let an unbelieving heart turn you away from the living God. Hebrews 3:13 (NIrV)

☐ CHAPTER SEVENTEEN

Memory Verse	Additional Memory Verses	
Then God said, "Let the earth be filled with animals, each producing more of its own kind. Genesis 1:24 (NCV)	For with God nothing will be impossible. Luke 1:37 (NKJV)	A person might think their own ways are right. But the Lord knows what they are thinking. Proverbs 21:2 (NIrV)

☐ CHAPTER EIGHTEEN

Memory Verse	Additional Memory Verses	
But since the beginning of the world those things have been easy to understand by what God has made. Romans 1:20 (NCV)	I am the way, the truth, and the life. No one comes to the Father except through Me. John 14:6 (NKJV)	Let the peace of Christ rule in your hearts. Colossians 3:15 (NIV)

BIBLE READING PLAN

This is a master list of the Bible reading found at the start of each chapter. This list also includes readings that do not appear in the chapter headings. For a printable version of this list, visit: www.hideandseekministries.com.

CHAPTER ONE	CHAPTER TWO
Bible Verses	**Bible Verses**
☐ Genesis 1 ☐ Genesis 2	☐ 2 Kings 6:1-23 ☐ John 3:1-21
Additional Bible Verses	**Additional Bible Verses**
☐ Ruth 1 ☐ Ruth 2 ☐ Ruth 3 ☐ Ruth 4	☐ Daniel 10 ☐ Acts 1 ☐ Acts 2 ☐ 2 Corinthians 5

CHAPTER THREE	CHAPTER FOUR
Bible Verses	**Bible Verses**
☐ Psalm 145 ☐ Psalm 146 ☐ Psalm 147	☐ Daniel 1 ☐ Daniel 2:1-23
Additional Bible Verses	**Additional Bible Verses**
☐ Exodus 1 ☐ Exodus 2 ☐ Exodus 3 ☐ Exodus 4	☐ Exodus 5 ☐ Exodus 6 ☐ Exodus 7 ☐ Exodus 8

CHAPTER FIVE	CHAPTER SIX
Bible Verses	**Bible Verses**
☐ Exodus 19 ☐ Psalm 19	☐ Luke 1:1-25 ☐ Luke 1:57-66
Additional Bible Verses	**Additional Bible Verses**
☐ John 1 ☐ John 2 ☐ Exodus 9 ☐ Exodus 10	☐ Exodus 11 ☐ Exodus 12 ☐ Exodus 13 ☐ Exodus 14

CHAPTER SEVEN	CHAPTER EIGHT
Bible Verses	**Bible Verses**
☐ Proverbs 1 ☐ Proverbs 2	☐ Psalm 1 ☐ Proverbs 3
Additional Bible Verses	**Additional Bible Verses**
☐ Mark 16 ☐ Matthew 28 ☐ Numbers 21 ☐ John 3	☐ Romans 3 ☐ Romans 4 ☐ Romans 5 ☐ Romans 6

CHAPTER NINE	CHAPTER TEN
Bible Verses	**Bible Verses**
☐ Proverbs 15 ☐ James 3	☐ Proverbs 4 ☐ Mark 4
Additional Bible Verses	**Additional Bible Verses**
☐ Numbers 13 ☐ Numbers 14 ☐ Numbers 15 ☐ Numbers 16	☐ Matthew 13 ☐ Matthew 14 ☐ Matthew 15 ☐ Hebrews 11

CHAPTER ELEVEN	CHAPTER TWELVE
Bible Verses	**Bible Verses**
☐ Genesis 3 ☐ John 8:31-47	☐ Ephesians 6:10-18 ☐ Luke 4:1-15
Additional Bible Verses	**Additional Bible Verses**
☐ Genesis 37 ☐ Exodus 32 ☐ Joshua 9 ☐ 1 Kings 21	☐ Mark 5 ☐ Mark 6:7-13 ☐ Mark 9:14-29 ☐ Mark 16

CHAPTER THIRTEEN	CHAPTER FOURTEEN
Bible Verses	**Bible Verses**
☐ Ezekiel 28:11-19 ☐ Psalm 8 ☐ Luke 10:1-20	☐ Ephesians 1 ☐ Ephesians 2
Additional Bible Verses	**Additional Bible Verses**
☐ John 14 ☐ Mark 14 ☐ Mark 15 ☐ Mark 16	☐ Luke 15 ☐ 2 Timothy 1 ☐ 2 Timothy 2 ☐ John 10:1-21

CHAPTER FIFTEEN	CHAPTER SIXTEEN
Bible Verses	**Bible Verses**
☐ Genesis 5 ☐ Psalm 148	☐ Genesis 6 ☐ Genesis 7
Additional Bible Verses	**Additional Bible Verses**
☐ 1 John 1 ☐ 1 John 2 ☐ 1 John 3 ☐ 1 John 4	☐ Genesis 8 ☐ Genesis 9 ☐ Genesis 11 ☐ Psalm 115

CHAPTER SEVENTEEN	CHAPTER EIGHTEEN
Bible Verses	**Bible Verses**
☐ Job 40 ☐ Job 41	☐ Romans 1
Additional Bible Verses	**Additional Bible Verses**
☐ Job 38 ☐ Job 39 ☐ Psalm 121 ☐ Proverbs 21	☐ Acts 3 ☐ Acts 4 ☐ Acts 5 ☐ Acts 6

NOTES

Chapter 4: The Power of God's Wisdom

[1] Clive Gifford, *Out of This World: All the Cool Stuff About Space You Want to Know* (London: Buster Books, 2011), p. 53.

[2] Clive Gifford, *Out of This World: All the Cool Stuff About Space You Want to Know* (London: Buster Books, 2011), 66.

[3] Giles Sparrow, ed., *Eyewitness Universe* (New York: DK Publishing, 2015), 54.

[4] Clive Gifford, *Out of This World: All the Cool Stuff About Space You Want to Know* (London: Buster Books, 2011), 54.

Chapter 5: The Power of God's Glory

[1] Job 38:4, 8, 12, 16, 18, 19, 22, 24, 25, 32-34, 39 (NIrV)

Chapter 6: The Power of God's Words

[1] "Why Bible Translation?" *Wycliff Bible Translators,* accessed May 30, 2017, https://www.wycliffe.org/about/why.

Chapter 15: Creation and Science, Part 1

[1] Gregory Parker et al., *Biology: God's Living Creation,* 2nd Edition (Pensacola: Pensacola Christian College, 1997), 358.

2 DeWitt Steele and Gregory Parker, *Science of the Physical Creation in Christian Perspective,* 2nd Edition (Pensacola: Pensacola Christian College, 1996), 73.

3 Gregory Parker et al., *Biology: God's Living Creation,* 2nd Edition (Pensacola: Pensacola Christian College, 1997), 360.

Chapter 16: Creation and Science, Part 2

1 DeWitt Steele and Gregory Parker, *Science of the Physical Creation in Christian Perspective,* 2nd Edition (Pensacola: Pensacola Christian College, 1996), 282-287.

2 DeWitt Steele and Gregory Parker, *Science of the Physical Creation in Christian Perspective,* 2nd Edition (Pensacola: Pensacola Christian College, 1996), 277-278.

Chapter 17: Creation and Science, Part 3

1 Rob Houston, ed., *Eyewitness Dinosaur* (New York: DK Publishing, 2014), 66.

2 James Strong, "The New Strong's Expanded Exhaustive Concordance of the Bible." In *The New Strong's Expanded Dictionary of the Words in the Hebrew Bible* (Nashville: Thomas Nelson Publishers, 2001), 300.

Chapter 18: No One Has an Excuse

1 Rich Deem. "Did Albert Einstein Believe in a Personal God?," *Evidence for God.* Last modified May 17, 2011. http://www.godandscience.org/apologetics/einstein.html

ABOUT HIDE AND SEEK MINISTRIES

Hide and Seek Ministries loves kids! HSM provides Christian resources for kids and their caregivers to help each one develop a personal relationship with God. Each child should know they are loved, valued, have a purpose, and know how to apply God's Word to their life. Founded by two experienced Christian teachers, HSM is a discipleship ministry that helps people around the world know how to follow and live for Jesus Christ. Find out more by visiting www.hideandseekministries.com.

www.hideandseekministries.com

HIDDEN TREASURE QUEST

An in-depth Christian discipleship series for ages nine to fourteen.

Search through the Bible as if you were on a quest for Hidden Treasure (Proverbs 2:1-11)

BOOKS IN THE SERIES INCLUDE:
1. Knowing God Through Creation

2. Knowing God Through Jesus

3. Knowing God Through the Holy Spirit

FIND OUT MORE AT:
www.hideandseekministries.com